The Official

GAME OF
THRONES

Cookbook

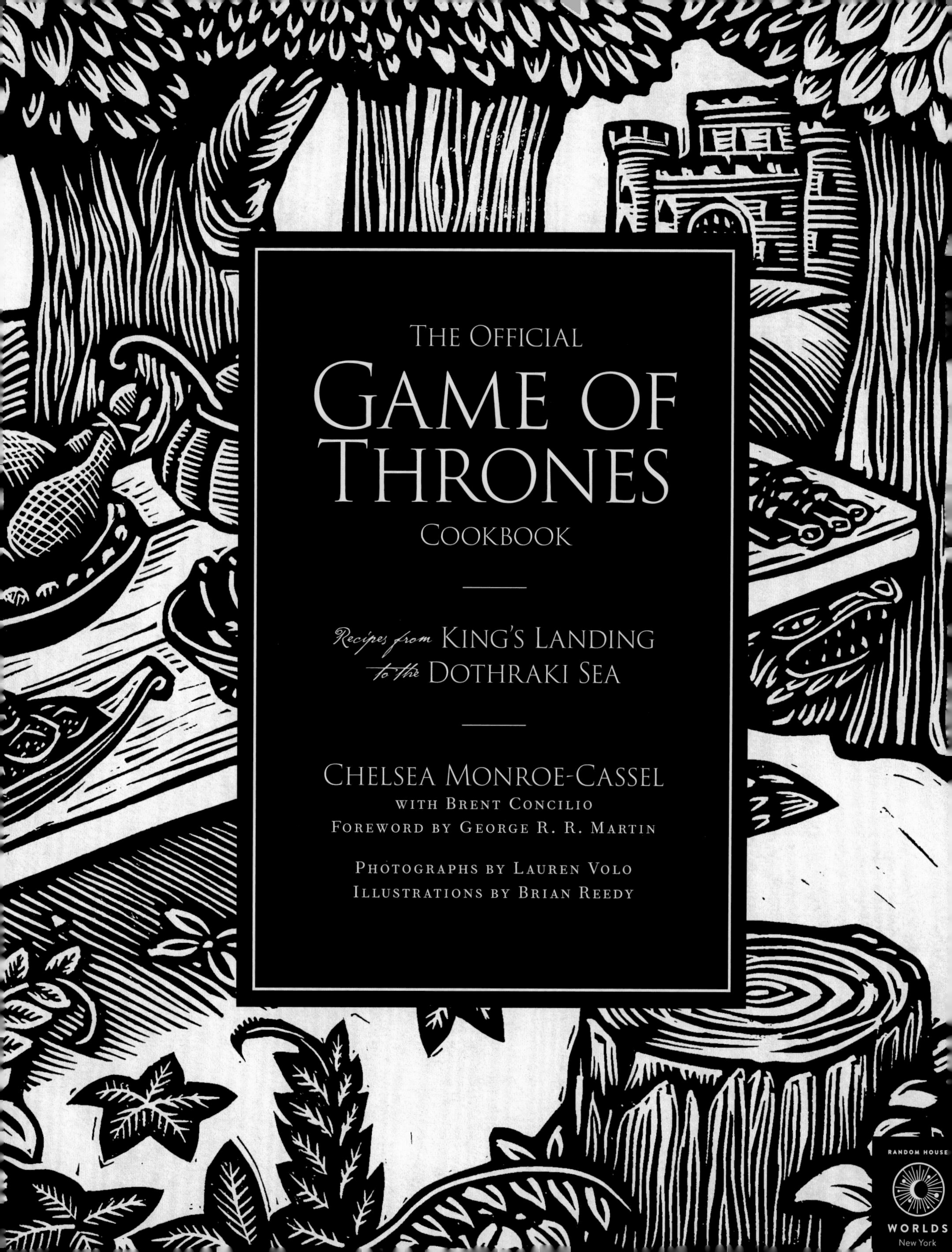

THE OFFICIAL

GAME OF THRONES

COOKBOOK

Recipes from KING'S LANDING
to the DOTHRAKI SEA

CHELSEA MONROE-CASSEL

WITH BRENT CONCILIO
FOREWORD BY GEORGE R. R. MARTIN

PHOTOGRAPHS BY LAUREN VOLO
ILLUSTRATIONS BY BRIAN REEDY

RANDOM HOUSE
WORLDS
New York

For Rafe, my little wolf.

*May you always have an appetite for
good food and adventure.*

Contents

Of course, I never did any of those things, not really. I only read about them. The experiences we have in books cannot possibly compare with the experiences of "real life." Real life is certainly more intense . . . *when we are living it*. When we are immersed in the moment, with all of our senses working. Yes, certainly.

Afterward, though—the next day, the next year, ten years later—perceptions can change. I was twelve or thirteen when I passed through the Mines of Moria with Gandalf and the Fellowship, but I still remember that experience vividly. An experience I never had. Yet I could not tell you what room I was in when I read those words, what day it was, whether I was in bed or in a chair, whether it was summer or winter, who my teacher was that year. It is Moria I remember, Moria that shaped me.

I love nothing more than opening a new book and falling through the pages. The tales that I love best are totally immersive. That's what I aspire to provide to my own readers as well. I want them to see the colors of the knights' surcoats in the tournament. I want them to hear the clash of steel on steel when swords cross, to hear the shrieks of dying men on the battlefield. If a song is sung, I want them to hear the words, get a sense of the rhythm. I want them to remember the sunsets, to glimpse fireflies in the dusk, to feel the heat of the dragon's fire. I want them to *live* my story, not just read it. When they sit down at my table, I want them to *taste the food*.

Nothing is gratuitous, as I see it. It is all part of the experience. If the plot is all that matters to you, well, there are Cliff's Notes you can read in a tenth the time.

Me, I will stay with novels—the richer and more immersive the better.

I hope you'll enjoy cooking the dishes within these pages. And I hope the taste of them will take you back to the first time you tasted them in the pages of *A Game of Thrones* or *A Storm of Swords* or (one day, I hope) *The Winds of Winter*. Pass the mead, please, and have a slice of dragon-roasted goat.

—*George R. R. Martin*

A Note on Modernization

By Chelsea Monroe-Cassel

Food is a way to share love and joy with others, to explore history and geography, and to travel from the comfort of our own homes to other realms. Some recipes are passports to faraway places to which we have never traveled; others are messages from the past, missives from a long line of cooks and eaters sending forward the dishes they value most. It is up to us to take those recipes, learn how to prepare them, and then pass them on, teaching our children to stir the dough and—occasionally—lick the spoon.

This curious collection of recipes is a journey in both space and time. Naturally, when I was asked by my publisher if I would undertake the modernization of an unusual manuscript found moldering among the stacks at Oldtown, I jumped at the opportunity. This mysterious folio represented a chance to dig into a unique culinary treasure, a record of a time and place we can only imagine.

Through considerable effort and laborious testing, I have fine-tuned these recipes to make them more accessible for modern readers, although I have been careful to maintain the voice of the original author, Maester Alton, including his accounts of each recipe's origin and relevant footnotes. Where helpful, I have added my own notes to aid readers with access to a modern kitchen and included suggested pairings to accompany the dishes.

What I hope you will find, as you leaf through this book, is a flavorful collaboration between me and Maester Alton. I hope you will imagine us together in the kitchen, surrounded by his scrolls and parchments, warmed by the oven and one another's company. May our combined efforts bring you joy, friendship, and a deeper understanding of the people and cultures of Westeros.

—Chelsea Monroe-Cassel

Introduction

By Maester Alton

very maester who spends his career not in service to some great lord but at the Citadel itself hopes for at least one of two accomplishments: to attain the rank of archmaester, surpassing all others in one of the twenty-one scholarly disciplines (represented by the wide array of metals that may appear in the links of a maester's chain), or to leave for posterity some great work—a piece of scholarship that lifts the Crone's Lantern and shines the light of knowledge on some previously unknown corner of the world, that those who come after may think on what we have learned and enter into dialogue with us even after our bones are dust and our names preserved only in the yellowed vellum of that celebrated manuscript.

For me, I know there will be no triple link, and no acolytes to call me "archmaester" in my dotage when my mind's best years are spent. The wisdom of the older archmaesters is oft honored more for the paths it cut in youth rather than the roads it is likely to open in the twilight years, when the edge of reason is dulled with sleep and insight clouded with dreams.

I flatter myself in thinking that *were* there a link for knowledge of meat and mead, my knowledge in that realm would long since have earned me the triple link and the honorific that I seem here to spurn with such bad grace, knowing it to be beyond my reach. No matter. Instead I leave behind me this manuscript, which I hope will one day be recognized as a useful inquiry into the foods of the Seven Kingdoms and beyond, and how those dishes reflect the places and the peoples who enjoy them.

I leave this missive as preface to what I regard as my life's greatest work, that you—future reader known only to me by our shared passion for the subject of this text—might understand what it is you hold in your hands. It is more than a mere collection of recipes; it is a history of Westeros and those invisible ties that bind us much closer than any of us realize to our neighbors across the narrow sea. It is a story of who we are.

But first, I will say a few things about who I am.

I was born in a time of peace, the only son of Ben Beesbury, Lord of Honeyholt. My youth was spent on the shores of the Honeywine, where I fashioned my dreams from the legends of old and the songs of traveling singers. I knew in my heart that I would master skill with sword and shield, and one day distinguish myself on the field of battle, bringing glory to my House.

But late in the reign of King Aegon V, the harvests were bountiful and summers long, and there was little need for famed warriors. Eventually, with time came temperance, and I arrived at the realization that I was not suited for a warrior's life. My accomplishments would be with a quill, not at the quintain, and words would be my weapons: I would be a knight of the mind.

I resolved to travel to the Citadel and forge a chain, despite the protestations of my father who had no other son to inherit lands and title, which instead passed to my cousin Warryn upon my father's death. Yet when I arrived, hungry for knowledge but lacking in direction, still I sought to distinguish myself with some great work. At first, I considered a treatise on the keeping of bees—a hobby of my youth more or less compulsory for those of my household—but it did not take long to learn that several other maesters, one of them my own grandfather's great uncle, had already written definitive works on the topic.

I took to wandering aimlessly through the shelves of the Citadel's vast library, pulling books and scrolls at random—searching, I suppose, for some sort of direction. I still remember the moment when I made the discovery. The recipe fragment I found was of brittle parchment, the ink scarcely legible apart from the words at the top: Cake of Limone. Instantly, I recalled the lemon cakes of my youth: delicate pastries in which sweet honey and sour citrus vied for dominance. My senses ignited with the remembered taste and smell, and there I stood in the stacks, mouth watering. So I found at long last the interest that would bloom into a life-long passion. To my knowledge, the study of the foods and drinks of Westeros has not yet been undertaken by any maester.

Shortly after this, Prince Rhaegar Targaryen came to the Citadel, seeking some scrap of lore in our archives. Like so many others, I was struck by his quiet intensity, his zeal for learning. And when he played his harp for us, I wept with the rest for the sheer beauty of it. This, I thought, was a future king worthy of whatever humble gifts I could offer. I threw myself into my research, compiling recipes with the intent of presenting my work as a coronation gift to Prince Rhaegar when he took up his father's crown.

But the gods laugh at the plans of men, and everything changed when Prince Rhaegar was felled at the Trident. All the kingdom's hope, and mine, was bound up in the beautiful prince who loved his books more than battle.

One thing was certain: no longer would a study of Targaryen cuisine be welcome at court. I confess that I became dispirited and set my work aside.

It was not until a colleague of mine in King's Landing, knowing my interest in the subject, secretly obtained and sent a packet of recipes from the Red Keep's kitchens, fearing their destruction in the upheaval surrounding Robert's Rebellion. Some of these recipes appeared to have come to Westeros with the Targaryens, and might provide the sole surviving glimpse into the foods enjoyed by the dragonlords of Old Valyria. Despite myself, my curiosity was once again piqued.

With the Citadel's vast archives at my disposal, I set to work again in earnest. This time, I sought out recipes that ought to be preserved as well as those that sparked my own personal interest. What could a food tell us about the people who ate it? What incredible dishes survived to our present day from ancient origins? Did any recipes survive the Doom of Valyria?

So I present to you, dear reader, the culmination of my life's work. What began as a regal gift has grown in scope to a record of the very identity of these Seven Kingdoms and the fiery past that forged us. I may never possess the mask, ring, and rod of an archmaester, but at least here, in these pages, I hope to be regarded as that which I set out to be so long ago in my youth: a knight of the mind.

Yours in service,
Maester Alton

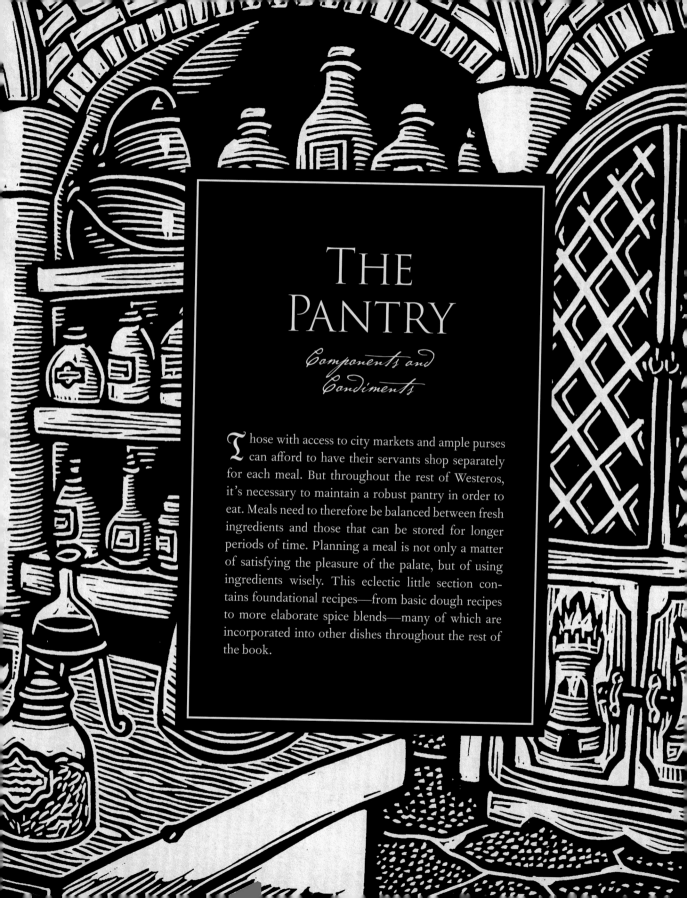

THE PANTRY

Components and Condiments

Those with access to city markets and ample purses can afford to have their servants shop separately for each meal. But throughout the rest of Westeros, it's necessary to maintain a robust pantry in order to eat. Meals need to therefore be balanced between fresh ingredients and those that can be stored for longer periods of time. Planning a meal is not only a matter of satisfying the pleasure of the palate, but of using ingredients wisely. This eclectic little section contains foundational recipes—from basic dough recipes to more elaborate spice blends—many of which are incorporated into other dishes throughout the rest of the book.

Mustard from Oldtown

MAKES: *About 2 cups*
PREP: *15 minutes*
INFUSING: *1 to 3 days*
PAIRS WELL WITH: *Ham or Boiled Beef (page 160);*
Sesame Rings (page 114)

Some healers will know mustard only for its warming qualities. When used as a poultice, it aids in the healing of injured muscles and aching joints, as well as in drawing out lingering congestion from a chest. But anyone who has studied at the Citadel could not miss the famed mustard blends made and sold in Oldtown. As such, I would be remiss if I did not include one such recipe in my collection. It is one of the flavors of my youth, as connected to my studies as the heady scent of flowers and fresh fruit that wends its way through the city streets.

After long spells at my studies, or perhaps a flagon of cider too many from the Quill and Tankard, this mustard was just the thing to restore me to my senses. It possesses a flavor so strong that it burns right up into the bridge of the nose, chased by a fiery kick on the tongue. Although the mustard is sealed into jars and sold around Westeros, nowhere else save Oldtown does it maintain that intensity, which mellows with age and travel. And a passion for the spicy spread has made its way to more than a few great houses along with their maesters, I'd warrant.

1 cup black or brown mustard seeds
½ cup almonds, chopped fine
½ cup pine nuts, chopped fine
1 to 2 teaspoons salt, to taste

Pinch of ground cumin
¼ cup honey, or to taste
1 cup cold water
½ cup lime juice or white wine vinegar

➤ GRIND THE MUSTARD SEEDS for a few seconds in a spice or coffee grinder, or by hand with a mortar and pestle; you want them mostly whole. Add the chopped almonds and pine nuts and grind the mixture into a paste. Transfer everything to a medium bowl and add the salt, cumin, honey, and cold water. Mix well and let stand for 10 minutes.

➤ POUR IN THE LIME JUICE and stir well. When everything has blended, pour the mixture into a glass jar, cover, and store it in the fridge. Wait at least 24 hours before using; it will continue to mellow the longer it sits. Mustard made this way will last several months in the fridge if kept covered.

Brown Butter Pastry Crust

MAKES: *1 batch*
PREP: *15 minutes*
USED IN: *White Harbor Meat Pie (page 148);*
Pease Pie Laced with Bacon (page 146); Cherry Tart (page 178)

Many cooks don't take the extra time to brown the butter for their crusts, but a few of the best know it enhances the flavors of both crust and filling. The baker in King's Landing from whom I learned this recipe was one such—a true master of the art, as is evidenced by the considerable demand for her pies in the streets and byways around the Old Gate. Accordingly, this has become my main recipe for pastry dough, with small changes depending on the type of pie. The resulting crust is flaky yet strong, with a subtle, almost nutty flavor that complements many fillings.

2 cups all-purpose flour   1 egg yolk
½ teaspoon salt   ⅓ cup water
6 tablespoons salted butter

➤ PLACE THE FLOUR AND SALT into a medium mixing bowl and set aside.

➤ MELT THE BUTTER in a saucepan over medium heat. Continue to cook for several minutes, and when it foams up, start to stir it. At this point, it will begin to quickly brown, so cook for another minute or so, until it is a nice rich brown color.

➤ REMOVE THE BUTTER from the heat and pour it into the bowl of flour. Add the egg yolk. Using a fork, toss everything together until no large pieces remain. The mixture should be relatively smooth but still fairly dry. Gradually mix in the water just a bit at a time, stirring until the dough comes together. Once the dough can be handled, turn it out onto a lightly floured surface and knead several times until you have a smooth lump of dough. Wrap and chill until ready to use.

Spice Blends

Freehold Spice Blend

MAKES: *About 2½ tablespoons*
PREP: *5 minutes*
USED IN: *Dragonstone Jaerhilla (page 97);*
Crown Roast of Boar's Ribs (page 157)

Legends state that some of the dragons of Old Valyria preferred their meat not only charred, but strongly seasoned as well. As appealing as I find it to imagine the dragons of old having favorite cooks, the only real evidence of such is the fragment of a damaged text, Galendro's *Fires of the Freehold*, that may itself be a mistranslation of an earlier work. Still, given the nearly unfathomable wealth and opulence of Old Valyria, it's certainly possible that thousands of pounds of spice mix were consumed daily by the Freehold's dragons. Regardless of the whimsical truth or rumor, a descendant of this spice blend can be found in nearly all of Valyria's daughter cities, albeit with regional nuances. Overall, the blend is richly warming, with a sharpness from several of the ingredients that lingers and builds with each bite.

1½ tablespoons smoked paprika
2 teaspoons ground cinnamon
1 teaspoon ground ginger

1 teaspoon ground sumac
½ teaspoon ground black pepper
½ teaspoon chili powder

➤ MIX TOGETHER THE SPICES and store in an airtight container for up to 6 months; the potency of the spices will fade over time, so the blend is best when reasonably fresh.

Old Ghis Spice Blend

MAKES: *About 2½ tablespoons*
PREP: *5 minutes*
USED IN: *Meereenese Soup with Ginger (page 92);*
Flaky Flatbread (page 122)

Because the Old Empire of Ghis predates the rise of Valyria by several thousand years, this spice blend may well be one of the oldest recipes in this collection. From the few accounts I could find, mostly shipping logs and trade accounts, the basic recipe for this blend has remained largely unchanged for millennia.

1 tablespoon ground turmeric
2 teaspoons ground cumin
½ teaspoon smoked paprika
1 teaspoon ground ginger
½ teaspoon chili powder

¼ teaspoon ground cinnamon
1 teaspoon garlic powder
Pinch of ground long pepper or
    ground black pepper

➤ MIX TOGETHER THE SPICES and store in an airtight container for up to 6 months; the potency of the spices will fade over time, so the blend is best when reasonably fresh.

Stag's Spice

MAKES: *About 4 tablespoons*
PREP: *5 minutes*
USED IN: *Seasoned Butter (page 34); Stewed Plums (page 175);*
Boiled Beef with Horseradish (page 160); Onion Broth with Carrot and Goat (page 94);
Cinnamon Swirled Loaf (page 132); Fried Fig Tarts (page 189)

One of the more common spice blends throughout the Seven Kingdoms, at least in noble houses, this mix can be used in everything from sweets to meaty main courses. I suspect that the current incarnation of this powder is a medley of seasonings first brought to Westeros by the Andals, and then developed further after the Targaryen conquest and the integration of Dorne introduced new spices and flavors. The subtle warming blend masks a kick of pepper that sharpens and enlivens other flavors in a dish.

2 tablespoons ground cinnamon
4 teaspoons ground ginger

4 teaspoons ground grains of paradise
½ teaspoon ground anise

➤ MIX TOGETHER THE SPICES and store in an airtight container for up to 6 months; the potency of the spices will fade over time, so the blend is best when reasonably fresh.

Mango Relish

MAKES: *About 2 cups*
PREP: *10 minutes*
COOKING: *45 minutes*
PAIRS WELL WITH: *cheeses; sweet white wines; fish dishes*

Archmaester Gallard, whose incomparable work *Children of Summer* gives us much of the history of the Summer Islanders, contends that food on the Islands is based on pleasure and celebration. This relish is common on vessels out of Lotus Point and Tall Trees Town, served as part of the luxuriant fare on which the Summer Islanders pride themselves aboard their so-called swan ships—meals which would put many a Westerosi captain to shame. The Velaryons apparently adopted some of this custom of sumptuous fare at sea, which might account for some of their success as a navy in the days of the old Targaryen kings. (I firmly believe that soldiers and seaman who eat better fight better, although I boast no iron link to establish my authority on such a matter.) The relish I describe below keeps well during long voyages at sea, and some Westerosi ingredients have found their way into the recipe after it reached Dragonstone.

Each bite of the relish bursts with flavors both exotic and common. The mangoes put one in mind of the sunny beaches of the Summer Isles, while the acidic bite of vinegar wars with the sweetness of both sugar and fruit. I found the depth of complexity in this relish almost astonishing for seemingly so simple a recipe. Yet it complements and enhances whatever it is served with, from cheese plates to whole braised fish and roasted meats.

1 cup sugar
½ cup white wine vinegar
2 large, ripe mangoes, peeled, pitted, and diced
½ red onion, diced
¼ cup diced dried apricots

¼ cup dried cranberries
1 tablespoon minced crystallized ginger
1 garlic clove, minced
1 teaspoon whole mustard seeds
Pinch of red pepper flakes

➤ COMBINE THE SUGAR AND VINEGAR in a medium saucepan over medium-high heat. Stir occasionally until the sugar dissolves. Add the remaining ingredients and turn the heat down to medium-low. Simmer, uncovered, for about 45 minutes, or until the fruit is softened and the liquid has mostly boiled away.

➤ THE RELISH CAN BE enjoyed as is, or pulsed in a food processor or with an immersion blender for a smoother texture. Keeps for several days, covered and refrigerated.

Rosehip Syrup

MAKES: *About 2½ cups*
PREP: *15 minutes*
COOKING: *20 to 30 minutes*
PAIRS WELL WITH: *yogurt; Barley Griddlecakes (page 54);*
Poor Knights (page 53); Winter Tea (page 217)

The greatest healers in Westeros can be found primarily among the maesters of the Citadel, and accordingly their services are rendered almost exclusively to the greatest lords of the Seven Kingdoms. It is left to the woods witches to tend to the simple folk of the Seven Kingdoms, whatever their affliction. The maesters oft distain the woods witches, but those wise women with whom I've conversed impressed me greatly with their knowledge of herb-lore. Indeed, I've met many an acolyte aspiring to a silver link whose knowledge pales by comparison.

One of the most common ingredients in the elixirs and potions of these rustic healers is dried rosehip. While the hips can be gathered from hedgerows all across Westeros, rosehip syrup in any great quantity comes predominantly from the Reach, where roses and all other fruits and flowers that are meet and good seem to flourish. The blooms that are not harvested to make rose water are left to fruit, and the hips plucked and dried for use in recipes such as this. The resulting syrup is a welcome addition to any larder, especially after autumn has drawn to a close and the syrup's deep earthy flavor brightens the darkness of winter. Commonly poured over griddlecakes and breakfast pastries, this syrup may also be blended with hot herbal infusions. Archmaester Ebrose has argued that rosehips, along with citrus fruits for those who can afford them, are beneficial for warding off the wasting sickness that afflicts so many during long winters and extended sea voyages.

1 cup dried rosehips, roughly chopped
1 cup water
1 cup apple cider

1 cinnamon stick
½ cup honey, or to taste

➤ **IN A MEDIUM SAUCEPAN,** combine the rosehips, water, apple cider, and cinnamon stick. Place over medium heat and bring to a simmer. Let cook for 20 to 30 minutes, until the rosehips have softened considerably. Remove the cinnamon stick and puree the liquid with an immersion blender until smooth. Stir in the honey to taste, and press through a fine sieve. Transfer the syrup to a large, clean bottle or jar and store, covered, in the fridge for up to 2 weeks.

MAESTER'S NOTE *As this recipe sometimes sets more like a jelly than a syrup, you may wish to store your creation in a wide-mouthed jar, rather than a bottle. To turn it back into a syrup, simply return the mixture to the pot with a little hot water to thin it down to a pourable consistency and serve warm. A pinch of ground ginger or clove may also be added for increased flavor, as is oft done in the North.*

Klihilla Sauce

MAKES: *½ cup*
COOKING: *20 minutes*
PAIRS WELL WITH: *soups and stews, sauces, and marinades*

This fish-based sauce can be found in every land over which the dragonriders of Old Valyria flew, which may imply that it was they who first popularized it. The traditional method of its preparation involves fermenting vast quantities of small fish layered with salt over a period of many months—a process that eventually transforms the fish into a savory liquid. The immense fermenting vats are typically located far from city centers, and considerably downwind. Although this authentic method is no doubt rewarding for those who have the time and means to undertake it, the recipe that I include here offers the benefit of a similar result in a mere sliver of the time. Dark in color, heavy on the salt, the fishy elements are balanced out by spicy pepper flakes and a splash of lime, creating a sauce so rich in flavor that a small amount gives a potent result.

One 8-ounce can sardines in water, drained	¼ teaspoon red pepper flakes
1 cup water	1 tablespoon lime juice
2 tablespoons soy sauce	1 teaspoon cornstarch

➤ COMBINE THE SARDINES, water, soy sauce, and red pepper flakes in a medium saucepan over medium heat. Cook for 15 minutes, until the sardines have broken up and the mixture is fragrant. Combine the lime juice and cornstarch in a separate bowl, then add to the sardine mixture. Cook everything for another minute or so, until the sauce has thickened somewhat, then remove it from the heat and strain it into a clean bottle. Use straightaway or seal and refrigerate for up to a week.

➤ A DASH OF THIS SAUCE enhances the flavor of soups and stews, sauces, and marinades. In places such as Braavos, it is sometimes also added to fine olive oil as a dip for bread.

Seasoned Butter

MAKES: *A little more than ½ cup*
PREP: *15 minutes*
PAIRS WELL WITH: *fresh bread; meats and fish; and so on*

Butter is a staple throughout Westeros, beloved by high- and lowborn alike. The smallfolk consume it either plain or salted, which helps with preservation especially in the heat of summer. In lordly homes, however, cooks often add herbs and spices that reflect the bounty or tastes of a particular region. In the Reach, the Beesburys often mix honey and spices with butter to be served with bread or poultry, while the westerlands prefer some variety of berry-butter, and in the Iron Islands, butter is sometimes even mixed with salt and seaweed. No doubt the iterations of this simple recipe are as varied as the Seven Kingdoms themselves. Those listed below are among my personal favorites. Each is unique and incredibly flavorful, as well as beautiful to look at on the table. And the preparation couldn't be easier: simply mix and store for later use. All are exceptional served with bread and breakfast griddlecakes, used to baste poultry or fish as it cooks, or served atop roasted meats.

½ cup (1 stick) unsalted butter, softened   *Regional ingredients, listed below*

➡ IN A MEDIUM MIXING BOWL or a stand mixer, blend together the butter and desired regional ingredients. Divide the butter into several parts, roll the parts into logs wrapped with parchment paper, and place in a freezer bag. Freeze the majority until ready to use. The rest should keep for a week or so in the fridge. Simply slice off a small part at a time and enjoy!

The North

¼ teaspoon smoked salt
¼ cup diced wild leeks
(or a combination of green onions and garlic)
Pinch of ground black pepper

The Reach

Generous pinch of sea salt
¼ cup honey
2 tablespoons colorful edible flower petals (such as calendula, cornflower, violets, sorrel, etc.)

Dorne

Generous pinch of sea salt
1 minced chili pepper of desired intensity,
Zest of ½ lemon

The Stormlands

Generous pinch of smoked salt
½ cup cooked diced mushrooms
1 to 2 garlic cloves, minced
Pinch of ground white pepper

The Vale

Pinch of sea salt
¼ cup pumpkin puree
3 tablespoons honey
½ teaspoon Stag's Spice (page 25)

MAESTER'S NOTE *Although flavored oils are generally preferred in Essos, butter seasoned with 1 tablespoon of either Freehold Spice Blend (page 24) or Old Ghis Spice Blend (page 25) is incomparable.*

Bone Broth

MAKES: *About 3 quarts*
PREP: *10 minutes*
COOKING: *4 to 24 hours*

A good cook must master not only the art of cooking, but also the art of husbandry; they must be stewards as well as artists. Just as a dutiful steward will save the ends of spent candles to be melted down and made anew, a prudent cook saves the bones of roasts and cooked fowl to be used again. Once all the meat has been consumed, the bones can then be simmered until they render up this savory broth. Nourishing and flavorful, this broth is generally superior to normal stocks and can be used as a base in countless soups and stews and fed to those who are unwell.

2 pounds beef bones (such as marrow, oxtail, ribs, etc.)
2 carrots, chopped
2 celery ribs, chopped
1 yellow onion, roughly chopped

1 cinnamon stick
1 fresh or dried bay leaf
2 tablespoons cider vinegar
Salt and ground black pepper

➤ PREHEAT THE OVEN to 450°F. Rinse the bones and pat them dry. Spread them out on a baking sheet and cook in the oven for 15 minutes. Then add the carrots, celery, and onion to the baking sheet and cook for another 20 minutes or so, until the vegetables are quite soft. Remove the baking sheet from the oven and transfer the bones and vegetables to a large stockpot. Add the cinnamon stick, bay leaf, and vinegar, then season with the salt and pepper and add water to cover.

➤ PLACE A LID ON THE POT and simmer for at least 4 hours and up to 24 hours, topping up the water as needed to keep the bones submerged and the level of liquid where it was when starting the recipe.

➤ WHEN DONE COOKING, strain the broth through a fine-mesh sieve into a clean bowl. If you wish, the fat may either be skimmed off immediately or, if chilling the soup, scraped off the top once cold. The broth will often gel as it chills, but simply rewarm it gently to use. The broth may be kept in the fridge for a few days, or frozen for up to 12 months.

Royal Dough

MAKES: *1 batch of dough*
PREP: *15 minutes*
RISING: *1 hour*
USED IN: *Cinnamon Swirled Loaf (page 132);*
Poppyseed Pastries (page 184); Fried Breadsticks (page 123)

In the far-flung regions of the Seven Kingdoms, one can still find vestiges of the ancient flours: rough grains or dried legumes coarsely ground between stones—laborious work, often done by hand. But it was likely the Andals who introduced windmilling techniques to Westeros, which made possible the finely ground flour used in the majority of bread making today. In highborn homes everywhere but the North, this staple is often further augmented with saffron, sugar, and either orange blossom water or rose water to produce "royal dough"—the primary ingredient in a variety of loaves, pastries, and rolls, enjoyed almost exclusively by those few who can afford them.

2 teaspoons sugar
Pinch of saffron threads
¾ cup warm water
2 teaspoons active dry yeast
3 cups all-purpose flour

Pinch of salt
¼ cup (½ stick) unsalted butter, melted
1 egg yolk
2 tablespoons orange blossom water or
rose water, optional

➼ IN A SMALL MORTAR AND PESTLE or spice grinder, grind together the sugar and saffron. Transfer to a medium mixing bowl and add the warm water and yeast, then let sit for about 5 minutes to activate while you begin the rest of the dough.

➼ COMBINE THE FLOUR WITH THE SALT in a large mixing bowl. Add in the melted butter, whisking with a fork to distribute evenly. Make a small well in the center of the mixture and add in the egg yolk and orange blossom water, stirring to combine. Mix in the yeast mixture and stir everything together.

➼ WHEN YOU HAVE A COHESIVE DOUGH, turn it out onto a lightly floured surface. Knead for at least 5 minutes, until the dough is pliable and smooth. Place the dough in a lightly greased bowl, cover with plastic wrap or a damp cloth, and allow to rise somewhere warm for 1 hour, until about doubled in size. Use as needed in other recipes. The dough can be made and allowed to rise in the fridge a day ahead of using, if needed.

Citrus Curd

MAKES: *About 1½ cups*
PREP: *5 minutes*
COOKING: *15 minutes*
PAIRS WELL WITH: *scones or biscuits; yogurt*

The Dornish climate is as hospitable for citrus fruits as it is inhospitable for much else. As such, lemons, limes, and blood oranges are among Dorne's most valuable exports, prized throughout the whole of Westeros. Even in Dorne itself, fruit is expensive, but the farther north one travels, the more dear the price becomes. Nevertheless, for practical reasons the majority of Dornish produce is not eaten fresh; instead, it's dried, used in the production of fire wine, or preserved in other ways. Citrus curds are among the most popular methods of conserving Dornish fruits, as they can easily survive long periods of transportation or be set by to be enjoyed during a long winter, when an infusion of southern sunshine is welcome in any Westerosi household.

1 cup sugar
Zest of 2 lemons (about 2 tablespoons) or other citrus (see Maester's Note)
4 egg yolks

½ cup lemon juice or other citrus juice
¼ teaspoon ground cinnamon (optional)
½ cup (1 stick) unsalted butter

➤ COMBINE THE SUGAR, zest, yolks, and lemon juice in a medium saucepan over medium heat. Beat together with a whisk and cook for about 10 minutes, until the mixture has thickened noticeably. Remove from the heat and stir in the butter until melted. If desired, strain through a mesh sieve for a perfectly smooth texture.

MAESTER'S NOTE *The whites from the eggs can be used in a variety of other recipes. This recipe can likewise be made with a variety of other citrus fruits in the same proportions as above, using the zest and juice of whichever fruits you prefer. Feel free to experiment according to what the markets have available.*

Variations

Instead of lemons and cinnamon, use one of these following citrus combinations:

Orange or Blood Orange: 1 or 2 oranges; ¼ teaspoon ground cardamom
Lime: 4 to 6 limes; ½ teaspoon ground ginger

Almond Milk

MAKES: *About 5 cups*
PREP: *35 minutes*
SOAKING: *12 hours (optional)*

The cultivation of milk and butter is common everywhere in Westeros, but it comes with considerable challenges. No other agricultural products are as labor-intensive to produce, and even under the best seasonal circumstances, livestock must be managed with great care in order to supply reliable yields. And yet there is one obstacle to reliable dairy production that outstrips all others: winter. If winter turns out to be longer than the Citadel predicted, animals may run out of fodder before they can be turned out onto the grassy fields in spring. Because cows only produce milk after they have calved, milk production is dramatically reduced as the herds are butchered to a much smaller size. Thank the Seven, then, for the almond. Grown in sprawling groves in more temperate Essos, the almond—and in particular its milk—takes the place of much dairy throughout Westeros's long winters.

This milk can be readily bought from many markets in the winter seasons, but it is more economical for large households to make it themselves. It can be drunk chilled or warmed, plain or with spices, and used in a bevy of cooking recipes to make a creamy sauce with a subtly deep flavor. Versatile enough for both desserts and savory dishes, this milk has even made an appearance in the occasional recipe for an almond cheese—something I'd like to attempt. This very basic recipe can be enjoyed plain as a beverage or warmed with spices such as in the Spiceflower Brew (page 209) from Braavos. It can also be used in a variety of other recipes to great success.

2 cups (about 10 ounces) raw almonds
6 cups water

Generous pinch of salt
Honey or sugar, to taste

➤ **IF YOU HAVE THE TIME,** soak the almonds in a bowl of water for around 12 hours to soften them, then drain them thoroughly. This will help extract more of the milk when you blend them (see Maester's Note below).

➤ **COMBINE THE ALMONDS** and 2 cups of the water in a food processor or blender, and blitz until the mixture looks like a thick paste. Continue adding the remaining water 2 cups at a time, processing after each addition until the almonds are ground very fine and you have a smooth-looking puree. Pour this mixture through a fine sieve or cheesecloth into a large bottle or pitcher, squeezing the cloth to bring out as much of the liquid as possible. Taste and sweeten to your preference, if desired. The almond milk will keep for several days, refrigerated, but may need to be shaken to remix if it settles before using.

➤ **THIS RECIPE PROVIDES** a good base to which can be added all manner of spice or flavorings, such as my personal favorite: a dash of pure vanilla extract.

MAESTER'S NOTE *The almonds will produce more milk if they are soaked for approximately half a day before processing. If you desire pure white meal for cooking, blanched almonds may be used, but I find the flavor of raw almonds slightly superior.*

CHELSEA'S NOTE *Save and dry the ground almonds for making Marzipan (page 191), or to be used in other baking recipes. To dry the almond meal, spread out the ground almonds on a baking sheet and cook at 180°F for a couple of hours, stirring and breaking up occasionally. This mixture can be further ground and stored in the freezer until needed.*

Breakfast

There is arguably no meal more important than a good breakfast: it wakes us up, fortifies us for travel or the day's labors, and generally sets the tone for the rest of the day. A simple porridge suffices for much of the populace, but those with access to sausage or bacon or even fried fish find that these proteins make a rewarding addition to the plate, as do hearty leftovers from the previous night's feasting. Fresh fruit when available, or preserves during the winter, provide a much-needed dash of sweetness.

Dothraki Dahanikh

MAKES: *2 servings*
PREP: *5 minutes*
COOKING: *About 20 minutes*
PAIRS WELL WITH: *yogurt; Cinnamon Swirled Loaf (page 132);*
Spiceflower Brew (page 209)

Maester Illister describes a porridge much like this one in his *Horse Tribes*, and I myself had the privilege of sharing just such a dish alongside a khalasar camped outside of Pentos. (The name, I am told, translates literally to "grass food.") The women of the khalasar harvest the grains from among the hundreds of grasses that make up the Dothraki sea, pulling the seedheads into satchels as they walk. It takes years of practice, I gather, to learn the art of pulling the grain while on the move. Once camped, the women beat the grasses to release the seeds, and use finely woven nesting baskets, or *qeso*, to separate the seeds from the chaff. The grass-seed is then combined with wildflower seeds and other ingredients to make a variety of stews, porridges, and even bread.

Because the harvesting process is so laborious, and presumably because the Dothraki sea is not entirely safe for those not under the protection of a khalasar, the grain has not gained popularity with the rest of Essos. A shame, in my opinion, for the porridge made with these seeds is incomparable and unlike anything in Westeros. Flavored with a variety of ingredients—depending on what "gifts" the khalasars have recently received from a city, or in trade in Vaes Dothrak—and sweetened with either honey or fruit molasses, this breakfast nourishes and braces one for a long day in the saddle.

1 cup whole teff grain
3½ cups boiling water
1 tablespoon unsalted butter
2 tablespoons chia seeds
1 tablespoon poppy seeds
½ teaspoon ground cinnamon

Pinch of ground cloves
½ cup chopped dried fruit, such as dates or
*   raisins, plus extra for serving*
Pinch of salt
¼ cup honey, plus extra for serving

➤ POUR THE TEFF into a medium saucepan over medium-low heat, and toast gently for 3 to 5 minutes, until it gives off a nice, nutty smell.

➤ ADD THE BOILING WATER, butter, chia seeds, poppy seeds, and spices. Bring the water to a simmer and stir occasionally to keep the porridge cooking evenly. After 10 minutes, add the chopped fruit, salt, and honey. Continue to cook for an additional 5 to 10 minutes, adding extra water if needed, until the porridge is cooked through to your liking. Scoop into serving bowls, and garnish with extra honey and dates.

MAESTER'S NOTE *The honey may be substituted with grape or pomegranate molasses, if available, for a deeper, richer flavor.*

Garlic Sausage Patties

MAKES: *About a dozen patties*
PREP: *10 minutes*
RESTING: *12 hours (optional)*
COOKING: *10 to 15 minutes*
PAIRS WELL WITH: *eggs; toast with jam; Boiled Beans with Bacon (page 77);*
Dothraki Pepper Beer Syrup (page 218)

I have long regarded garlic as among the greatest gifts nature has given man, both for its medicinal properties and its culinary merits. Because these papery bulbs flourish anywhere, they are as common in elaborate sept gardens as they are in simple plots of cultivated land beside the most humble of cottages. Smallfolk and highborn alike appreciate garlic for its ability to impart strong flavors to anything from simple broths to richer dishes of meat and vegetables.

These sausage patties are easy and quick to prepare. They sizzle when they hit the pan, and transform in a matter of minutes from raw meat to richly flavored discs that are an ideal accompaniment to any breakfast spread. With garlic at the fore, followed by the herbs, these patties cook to a crisp brown on the outside, while the inside remains tender. I personally enjoy them with eggs and a small beer of the darker variety, popular in the North.

1 pound ground pork, or a combination of
   ground pork and veal
6 to 8 garlic cloves, peeled and pressed
½ teaspoon dried sage
½ teaspoon summer savory

½ teaspoon salt
Pinch of ground black pepper
½ cup grated Parmesan cheese
1 to 2 tablespoons olive oil

➤ **IN A SMALL MIXING BOWL,** mix together the pork, garlic, herbs, salt, pepper, and Parmesan cheese (see Maester's Note). Cover and allow to sit in the refrigerator for about 12 hours for the flavors to reach their full potential; it's ideal if you can prepare the mix the night before you intend to serve it.

➤ **TO COOK THE SAUSAGE,** form the pork mixture into a dozen patties about 3 inches across and approximately ½ inch thick. In a large frying pan over medium heat, add the oil and cook the patties until nicely browned on both sides.

MAESTER'S NOTE *To further enhance the flavor, consider adding a splash of Klihilla Sauce (page 32).*

Poor Knights

MAKES: *About 4 servings*
PREP: *5 minutes*
COOKING: *15 minutes*
PAIRS WELL WITH: *Citrus Curd (page 42);*
maple syrup, jam, or honey; Seasoned Butter (page 34)

As a child at Honeyholt, I often broke my fast on a meal such as this—a simple dish called "Poor Knights" throughout much of Westeros. My mother used to line up the strips of battered and fried bread for me in little rows, like troops in an army, which I could then dip in honey from our hives. It was only when I was a man grown that I thought to wonder about the origin of their name. I could find nothing conclusive in my research, although as the recipe calls for a stale loaf, the name might have originated from knights counting coppers to buy day-old bread.

This simple yet satisfying breakfast makes use of slices of bread past their best. By immersing the stale bread in cream and eggs, it is transformed from something forgotten to something wonderful. The hint of spice adds flavor rather than warmth, slightly enhancing the overall taste of the bread. The real pleasure comes with dipping the slices in your choice of sauce. I was always partial to spiced honey, but some prefer citrus curd or jam.

Butter, for the pan
1 cup heavy cream, gently warmed
3 eggs
¼ teaspoon ground nutmeg

2 tablespoons sugar
8 (or more) slices of bread of your choice,
*   stale or lightly toasted*

➤ SET A LARGE FRYING PAN over medium heat and melt about a tablespoon of butter to coat the pan.

➤ IN A SMALL MIXING BOWL, rapidly beat together the heavy cream, eggs, nutmeg, and sugar for about a minute. Dip the bread into the bowl one or two slices at a time until both sides of the bread are coated. The bread should be soaked, but not falling apart.

➤ DEPENDING ON THE THICKNESS of the slices, fry the bread in the hot pan for 2 to 4 minutes per side, or until the bread is cooked through. Move to a cutting board and slice the bread into strips, then melt another tablespoon of butter in the pan and repeat the dredging and frying process until all the bread is used up. Dip the strips into your choice of sauce, such as honey or maple syrup.

MAESTER'S NOTE *Stale bread is best for this recipe, although lightly toasted bread may be used in a pinch. Some of the noble houses in the Reach also sprinkle the knights with rose water before serving.*

Barley Griddlecakes

MAKES: *About a dozen*
PREP: *5 minutes*
RISING: *30 minutes*
COOKING: *15 minutes*
PAIRS WELL WITH: *maple syrup, honey, or jam; bacon or sausage;*
Seasoned Butter (page 34); Rosehip Syrup (page 30)

I can think of few dishes more evocative of a crofter's cottage than these simple griddlecakes. My extensive travels occasionally leave me between cities and towns, with no formal lodging save small houses scattered amongst the sprawling fields. More often than not, the crofters or farmers are happy to exchange some food and a place by their fire for my herblore or culinary knowledge. And at most hearths, I have received some form of griddlecake.

In the spring, fresh herbs can be minced and added to the batter before frying, but I find this simpler version eminently satisfying. The slight tanginess of the goat cheese complements the earthiness of the barley. I most enjoy these griddlecakes topped with a little tart berry jam, and perhaps a little whipped cream if I am feeling extravagant and the seasons allow.

1 cup warm water
2 tablespoons honey
2 teaspoons instant dry yeast
1 egg

2 ounces goat cheese
Pinch of salt
1½ cups barley flour
Butter, for the pan

➤ COMBINE THE WATER, honey, and yeast in a small bowl, and set aside. In a larger mixing bowl, beat together the egg, goat cheese, and salt. Add the yeast mixture to this, then briskly beat in the barley flour until you have a smooth mixture. Cover the bowl loosely with a towel and allow the batter to sit at room temperature for about 30 minutes.

➤ LADLE SMALL AMOUNTS of the batter into a frying pan over medium heat, coated with a little melted butter, spreading the batter out a little to help it cook. Make a few griddlecakes at a time, depending on the size of your pan, cooking on each side for a minute or so until slightly browned, then flipping.

➤ SERVE WARM with the topping of your choice.

Gravy-Poached Eggs

MAKES: *4 servings*
PREP: *5 minutes*
COOKING: *10 minutes*
PAIRS WELL WITH: *toasted bread, such as Jaedo Havon (page 128);*
Boiled Beans with Bacon (page 77)

Versions of this breakfast are popular throughout the Seven Kingdoms, including in Old-town, where the Quill and Tankard serves a version made with gull eggs that I remember fondly. Novices of the Citadel who occasionally indulge in a night of heavy revelry universally agree that there is no better remedy for an evening of excess than a bit of eggs and gravy at the "Pen and Pint," as they have nicknamed the Quill and Tankard. Nevertheless, the best version of this dish I have ever encountered was served to me one morning at an inn on the road to Winterfell. The cook there was kind enough to provide me with his recipe, which is the one that I have included here.

The warm yolk of the egg, when broken, mixes with the savory gravy to produce a truly incomparable flavor, and the creamy consistency of this mixture provides a delightful base for the lightly spiced meat. A serving of toasted bread finishes the preparation to perfection.

4 eggs
4 slices toasted bread, for serving
3 tablespoons unsalted butter
3 tablespoons all-purpose flour
4 cups chicken broth or other broth, warmed
Pinch of ground mace

Pinch of ground nutmeg
Pinch of ground cloves
½ cup shredded leftover roast chicken or
  finely ground cooked sausage
Salt and ground black pepper

➼ BEGIN BY CRACKING THE EGGS into four small bowls, which will make them easier to poach later in the gravy. Set these aside and place the toasted bread on your serving plates.

➼ MELT THE BUTTER in a medium saucepan over medium heat and whisk in the flour. Let this cook for about 1 minute, until the mixture is golden brown and gives off a slight nutty aroma. Gradually whisk in the broth until the mixture has thickened somewhat, then add in the spices and the meat.

➼ USING A LARGE SPOON, make 4 small divots in the gravy, and pour an egg into each one. Using the same spoon, gently spoon the gravy over the top of each egg so that they cook on top as well as underneath. The eggs will be finished after only a few minutes, when the white is set and the yolk is still soft.

➼ WHEN THE EGGS ARE DONE, scoop them out of the pan one at a time, along with a generous portion of the meaty gravy, and place atop the toast. Season with salt and pepper.

Thick Cream of Wheat
with Honey and Butter

MAKES: *About 4 servings*
PREP: *5 minutes*
COOKING: *20 minutes*
PAIRS WELL WITH: *honey, maple syrup, or jam; berries; nut butter;*
Spiceflower Brew (page 209)

Some version of this dish is likely as old as the practice of cultivating grain in Westeros. The concept is simple: take the rough-ground berries of wheat and boil them into a thick porridge. The first to attempt such a recipe may well have been a goodwife tired of painstakingly grinding the wheat by hand into flour, which would then need to be baked into something else. Far easier and quicker is to simply boil it up and be done with it.

More lavish morning tables might include versions of this recipe tinged a rich golden color with saffron, but many content themselves with a lighter yellow hue from the addition of an egg yolk. Whatever your fancy, this dish provides a robust and filling start to a morning, and can be supplemented with a wide variety of additional ingredients or toppings. I personally prefer mine topped with a dollop of fresh butter and a generous drizzle of honey, but I've also enjoyed it heaped with fresh berries.

1½ cups almond milk, store-bought or homemade (page 44), warmed
Pinch of saffron threads
½ cup wheat berries, ground fairly fine
1 cup water
Pinch of salt
1 egg yolk
Butter, for serving
Honey or sweetener of choice, for serving

➤ IN A SMALL BOWL, combine ½ cup of the almond milk with the saffron and set it aside to steep.

➤ COMBINE THE WHEAT, water, the remaining 1 cup almond milk, and the salt in a small saucepan set over medium heat. Cook for about 15 minutes, or until the mixture is thick and the wheat has softened. Stir in the almond milk and saffron mixture and cook for another minute or so. Add in the egg yolk, stirring vigorously to combine. Cook for 1 to 2 more minutes, then remove from the heat. The cream of wheat is best served hot, but can be prepared ahead of time and reheated as well. Serve with a dollop of butter and honey.

CHELSEA'S NOTE *The wheat berries may be effectively ground to a fairly fine meal—similar to the consistency of coarse bread crumbs—using a coffee grinder, which will result in a much quicker preparation. A savory version of this recipe may also be made using less finely ground wheat and a beef or chicken broth in place of the water. Such a version is excellent served alongside venison.*

Oaten Porridge
with Cheese

MAKES: *2 to 4 servings*
PREP: *5 minutes*
COOKING: *25 minutes*
PAIRS WELL WITH: *strong tea; biscuits and jam; breakfast meats*

I happened on this savory porridge at an inn north of the God's Eye, where I stopped for a night during my first and only journey to the Wall. It was early in the autumn, and the air was already taking on the crisp chill that makes a man long for a hot drink and the smell of roast meat. The evening meal was unmemorable, but when I woke in the morning I was pleasantly surprised to find a steaming cauldron on offer in the common room. Much more elaborate than the everyday porridge we are all accustomed to, this oatmeal incorporates bits of meat and cheese that help fortify a traveler for long leagues in the chill air.

After a bit of cajoling, the proprietress, one Mistress Heddle, shared this recipe with me. As is sometimes the case with good food, the ingredients are quite simple: some oats, hearty stock, cheese, and a bit of ham. The resulting dish warms deep down to the bones from the first bite, a most welcome characteristic as the seasons turn. The oats soften as they cook, turning the water to a thick gruel made creamy by the addition of the cheese. The occasional bite of ham makes this simple rustic dish feel like a rich indulgence.

3½ cups beef stock
1 cup steel-cut oats
½ cup (2 ounces) cubed ham

½ cup shredded cheddar cheese
Salt and ground black pepper

➤ BRING THE STOCK TO A BOIL in a large saucepan, and add the oats. Reduce the heat to medium-low, add the ham, put the lid on, and cook for around 25 minutes, stirring occasionally to keep the oatmeal from sticking.

➤ WHEN THE TIME HAS ELAPSED, check the oats to see if they are soft and have absorbed all of the stock. If not, add a little more water and continue to cook until the oats are soft and all the stock is absorbed. Remove from the heat and stir in the cheese. Season to taste with the salt and pepper, and serve warm.

Braavosi Pepperfish

MAKES: *2 servings*
PREP: *10 minutes*
COOKING: *5 minutes*
PAIRS WELL WITH: *Olive Loaf (page 125);*
Dōnor Vīgilla (page 219) or watered wine

When traveling, I have always had a fondness for the sounds and smells of breakfast cooking. Nothing conveys the fresh potential of a new day like the tantalizing aroma of a morning meal, and few things convey a better sense of place than the contents of said repasts. I can still remember the first time I awoke as a novice in Old Town to the smell of bread hot from the ovens and the call of river gulls. It makes me smile even now. But rarely have I been anywhere with such a rich cacophony at the dawn hour as in Braavos, where pepperfish sizzle in hot oil and netters cry the morning catch.

These little fish are much celebrated when they appear in the markets, usually as winter is beginning in earnest. It's thought that the cold weather drives them eastward, into the nets of the Braavosi fisherfolk, who happily convey them back into the city's port at dawn's first light. The Braavosi love these little sardines breaded and fried until the outer skin cooks up to a crispy texture that crunches admirably. The pepper soaks into the fish as they cook, melding with the tender, flaky meat for a perfect finish. After a night of heavy reveling, as during the festival to mark the Uncloaking of Uthero, many partygoers pair their pepperfish with crusty bread and watered wine to ease them back into wakefulness.

½ cup cornmeal
¼ cup all-purpose flour
1 tablespoon salt
4 fresh sardines, cleaned and gutted

1 cup olive oil
½ teaspoon red pepper flakes, plus more
  to taste
Lemon or lime wedges, for serving

➤ IN A SMALL BOWL, combine the cornmeal, flour, and salt. Dip the sardines in this mixture, making sure to cover thoroughly.

➤ IN A SKILLET OR FRYING PAN, combine the olive oil and red pepper flakes. Bring to medium-high heat, and add the sardines. Flip the fish occasionally, and cook for several minutes, until both sides are a nice golden brown. Remove to a plate, sprinkle with the citrus juice, and serve warm.

MAESTER'S NOTE *If you find yourself away from a port, you may use whole sardines that have been packed into vessels for export. The flavors might not be quite so fresh, but I've found it to still be delicious. Simply pat the fillets dry before frying. For a spicy twist, consider adding a few tablespoons of chili-infused oil to the olive oil before frying the fish.*

Sides, Starters & Snacks

Whether you are after a smaller meal, a snack, or something with which to build out a full meal, look no further. These enticing recipes range from simple to exotic, and pair with a wide variety of dishes. Although common folk often dine on a single dish, in great houses, meals consist of at least one main course and a variety of other adjacent foods and smaller plates. This is both for the pleasure of the palate—as it's more enjoyable to eat a wide variety of flavors than a single one—as well as to demonstrate one's access to resources. A diversity of dishes is a statement of power, even though most great lords don't think of their dining habits as indications of their social status or political reach. The fact of the matter is that the way we dine in Westeros reflects the realities of our social structure. Nevertheless, carefully selected side dishes can bring life, flair, and variety to a table.

Pentoshi Curried Mushrooms

MAKES: *4 small servings*
PREP: *5 minutes*
COOKING: *20 minutes*
PAIRS WELL WITH: *toasted slices of rustic bread, such as Olive Loaf (page 125);*
Boiled Beef with Horseradish Sauce (page 160)

The range of mushrooms and spices available in Pentos is as varied as the diverse people who pass through this port city for business or pleasure, so it is no wonder the two ingredients have been so successfully wed. This dish is a popular offering in the taverns that open only after nightfall, where bravos vie to see who can endure the hotter spice in savory duels that are considerably less deadly than those with swords. Another variety of round, fat mushrooms is pickled with similar spices and loaded into the galleys of ships bound for distant ports, and many nobles send a servant running to the markets the moment they open in order to secure the freshest fungi of the day. In short, mushrooms are synonymous with the cuisine of Pentos.

This recipe is far from the hottest versions of this dish, but it nonetheless turns out a richly flavored side that is redolent with fine spices. The mushrooms are cooked until soft in a mixture of butter and garlic, then simmered in a seasoned broth. Plump golden raisins balance the flavors with a sweet counterpoint. Tradition amongst the smallfolk of Pentos holds that a silver coin, if boiled in the same pot as unknown mushrooms, will turn black if the fungi are poisonous. A quaint notion, but one not borne out by evidence, as I'm sure more than a few have discovered the hard way. One might surmise this anecdote may be as much about a peasant's wish to have a little silver to spare as it is purported culinary advice.

2 tablespoons unsalted butter
1 tablespoon olive oil
2 garlic cloves, minced
10 ounces baby bella mushrooms (12 to
    15 mushrooms), cleaned and sliced

½ teaspoon curry powder
½ cup chicken broth
¼ cup golden raisins
Salt and ground black pepper

➤ MELT THE BUTTER with the olive oil in a large saucepan over medium heat. Cook the garlic for several minutes, until golden and fragrant. Stir in the mushrooms to coat them with the butter, then let them cook for 10 minutes or so, until the mushrooms are soft and have soaked their juices back up.

➤ ADD THE REMAINING INGREDIENTS and allow to cook for another 5 minutes or so, until most of the liquid has been absorbed and the raisins are plump. Season with salt and pepper and serve warm.

Redwyne Roasted Grapes

MAKES: *About 4 servings*
COOKING: *20 minutes*
PAIRS WELL WITH: *soft baked cheese; Ironborn Ship's Biscuits (page 136);*
Tenderloin Skewers (page 165)

While grapes are grown in abundance throughout the Reach, the Arbor is known far and near for its prolific yields of the highest quality fruits for both wine and the table. The Redwynes are famed for their ability to coax additional harvests from their vineyards, and I learned part of their secret when I visited a childhood friend at the Arbor one summer. After each picking, they cut back the vines to trick the plants into thinking it is winter, thereby forcing them into a sort of dormancy. After such a period, the vines spring back to life and produce another crop. This process may be repeated several times so long as the summer lasts.

I discovered this deceptively simple dish during my first visit to the Arbor, when I was fortunate enough to observe the harvest firsthand. During a midday break for lunch, bunches of fresh grapes were spread over hot braziers along with the day's meat. This method of preparation enhances the inherent sweetness of grapes still on the vine, rendering them almost soft enough to spread, as though they are halfway to becoming jelly. The roasting grapes give off a smell of caramelized sugars when they are ready, tantalizing to the nose. The tiny acidic kick of the vinegar and the dash of salt and pepper round out the flavors, combining to create a dish considerably more complex than even the finest Arbor grapes on their own.

1 pound grapes
1 tablespoon olive oil
1 tablespoon balsamic vinegar

½ teaspoon coarse salt
Pinch of freshly ground black pepper

➤ PREHEAT THE OVEN to 350°F and place the grapes on a large, rimmed baking sheet. Drizzle with the olive oil and balsamic vinegar, then roast for about 20 minutes, until the grapes are somewhat wrinkled and sizzling. Sprinkle them with the salt and pepper and serve while warm.

MAESTER'S NOTE *The grapes can be roasted equally well on or off the vine, but I find if I plan to use them for another dish—as, say, a garnish or atop porridge—I prefer roasting them off the vine. This will make using them much more straightforward.*

Honey Roasted Chickpeas

MAKES: *4 to 6 servings*
PREP: *20 minutes*
COOKING: *30 minutes*
PAIRS WELL WITH: *beer or ale, such as Dothraki Pepper Beer Syrup (page 218);*
Redwyne Roasted Grapes (page 68)

This popular snack may have traveled to Dorne from across the narrow sea, but it does not seem to have originated with the Rhoynar themselves. It was likely introduced by sailors on trading cogs bound from coastal cities in Essos, where crunchy chickpeas are immensely popular in dockside taverns. There, they come in a variety of flavors and are more heavily salted—likely as a bid to keep thirsty sailors drinking the tavern's ale.

This version is somewhat sweeter with more mellow spices, and is enjoyed by nearly all tiers of Dornish society. The chickpeas are roasted until crisp, then coated in honey and spices before they are returned to the oven. They keep their crunchy texture remarkably well in the dry heat of the desert, which makes them a popular addition to the platters set out for afternoon meal. They are also popular among traveling merchants, as a bag of roasted chickpeas is light and can be affixed to a saddle for easy access on the road.

3 tablespoons honey
1 tablespoon olive oil
1 teaspoon salt
1 teaspoon ground cinnamon

½ teaspoon smoked paprika
Two 15-ounce cans chickpeas
½ teaspoon chili powder, or to taste

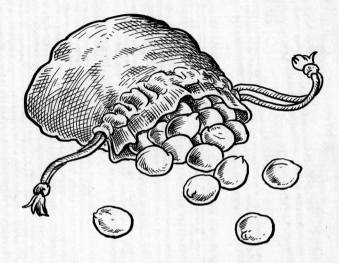

➤ **PREHEAT THE OVEN** to 400°F. Combine the honey, oil, salt, and spices in a medium mixing bowl and set aside.

➤ **DRAIN AND RINSE** the chickpeas, then rub off and discard their outer skins and dry the chickpeas completely with paper towels. Spread them out evenly on a large, rimmed baking sheet. Roast them in the oven for about 20 to 25 minutes, shaking the pan once about halfway through, until the chickpeas audibly rattle around on the pan.

➤ **POUR THE HOT CHICKPEAS** into the spiced honey mixture and stir until the chickpeas are evenly coated. Return them to the pan, spread them out, and bake them for another 5 minutes, until they sort of rattle on the baking sheet when shaken. Let the chickpeas cool for at least 10 minutes before transferring them to a serving bowl, breaking up any larger clumps as needed.

MAESTER'S NOTE *For a more exotic version, as from Essos, substitute the olive oil with toasted sesame oil, and the cinnamon and paprika with 2 teaspoons Old Ghis Spice Blend (page 25).*

Dressed Greens
with Apples and Pine Nuts

MAKES: *4 servings*
PREP: *20 minutes*
PAIRS WELL WITH: *Creamy Chestnut Soup (page 100);*
sparkling white wine

Salads are one of the bright highlights of our long and glorious Westerosi summers, when the fields are bountiful and the crops are plentiful. During this heady season of warmth and sunlight, fresh fruits and greens can be combined in endless, delightful ways to suit any table or occasion. This particular dish is popular in the Reach, where sweet apples and pomegranates grow in abundance.

Apples are sliced into thin rounds, then restacked in their original shape, each layer interspersed with a creamy cheese that serves as a textural counterpoint to the crunch of the fruit. Toasted pine nuts and pomegranate seeds provide little bursts of color and flavor, while a tangy dressing poured over the top finishes the dish to perfection. It's an easily prepared salad that is nonetheless bound to impress.

4 cups mixed spring greens
4 apples
2 to 4 tablespoons (1 to 2 ounces) crumbly
   cheese (such as feta, chèvre, or blue)
¼ cup toasted pine nuts

¼ cup pomegranate seeds
3 tablespoons honey, warmed
2 teaspoons balsamic vinegar
Pinch of freshly ground black pepper or
   ground grains of paradise

➤ DIVIDE THE GREENS EVENLY between four small plates. Slice the apples one at a time into rounds about ¼ inch thick or even thinner, cutting out the seeds and core from each slice. Stack these slices on the plated greens, interspersing a little cheese in between each layer to reconstruct the apple from the bottom up. Repeat the process with the remaining apples, then top everything with a bit more cheese, a sprinkle of the nuts, and the pomegranate seeds.

➤ IN A SMALL BOWL or jar, combine the honey and balsamic vinegar, stirring or shaking vigorously to combine them, then pour this dressing over the salads. Sprinkle with pepper and serve with sharp knives to cut the apples.

MAESTER'S NOTE *I've seen a similar salad served in Dorne, with slices of peeled blood orange in place of the apples, and a splash of sesame oil in the dressing.*

Pentoshi Buttered Parsnips

MAKES: *4 servings*
PREP: *5 minutes*
COOKING: *20 minutes*
PAIRS WELL WITH: *Flaky Flatbread (page 122);*
Pease Pie Laced with Bacon (page 146)

In Westeros, parsnips are a practical crop cultivated primarily because they keep well in winter and their preparation is a simple affair. In the North especially, parsnips are stored in great quantities to be mashed, boiled, or baked when the snow flies. However, across the narrow sea, a milder climate has afforded cooks the luxury of taking a more creative approach when preparing this humble vegetable. This has led to a number of dishes that emphasize the subtle sweetness of the root, rather than its utility.

The dish that I have included in this collection is one such—a selection from Pentos, where the addition of a few exotic ingredients transforms the parsnip from rustic to exotic. The Pentoshi roast the roots until soft, then coat them with rich spices and toss them with dried dates. Among the spices is turmeric, which imparts a vivid yellow tone that seems to make the parsnips glow, while a bit of ginger provides a gentle warmth. These flavors are further balanced with a touch of lemon and creamy yogurt.

1 pound parsnips
3 tablespoons unsalted butter, melted
1 teaspoon lemon juice
1 teaspoon ground ginger

½ teaspoon ground turmeric
½ cup pitted, diced dates
¾ cup Greek yogurt

➤ PREHEAT THE OVEN to 375°F and set out a large baking sheet.

➤ PEEL THE PARSNIPS, cutting away any woody interior of the larger parsnips to avoid bitterness. Cut into bite-size pieces and move to the baking sheet. In a small bowl, combine the butter with the lemon juice and spices, then drizzle over the parsnips. Toss the parsnips until they are completely covered, then spread out in a single layer.

➤ BAKE THE PARSNIPS for 15 minutes, then add the dates and return to the oven for another 5 minutes. Toss with the yogurt just before serving.

Boiled Beans
with Bacon

MAKES: *4 servings*
PREP: *10 minutes*
COOKING: *About 2 hours*
PAIRS WELL WITH: *toasted bread and sharp cheese; ale;*
meaty main courses such as Boiled Beef with Horseradish Sauce (page 160)

Various iterations of this dish can be found throughout much of our realm, from the camp-fires of the lowliest hedge knight to the halls of the greatest lords—especially when the winter winds sing and richer fare is in short supply. The special virtue of beans is that they absorb the flavors of whatever they are cooked with most efficiently. I've encountered a spicy variant of this dish in Dorne, a sweeter version in the Reach, one with exotic spices in King's Landing, and a version in the North that involves simmering the beans for hours in thick dark ale. Although boiled beans are not exclusively a seasonal dish, they are less popular in the late spring, after having been served so frequently during the colder months.

The recipe listed here is something of a simpler combination of several versions I have encountered and is easily adaptable to personal taste. Boiled for several hours, the beans swell until near bursting as they absorb the rich flavors from the onion, bacon, and savory broth. The mixture cooks until quite soft, just shy of the beans breaking down completely, resulting in a consistency that can easily be spread on toast or enjoyed as a side dish. Versatile enough to be served from breakfast to supper, this deceptively simple dish will feel at home on any table, and the recipe is infinitely adaptable depending on both climate and region.

3 bacon strips, diced
1 yellow onion, diced
2 garlic cloves, minced
1 cup small, dried legumes, such as pinto
   beans or black-eyed peas

2 carrots, chopped
1 bay leaf
6 cups chicken or vegetable broth
Salt and ground black pepper

➤ ADD THE BACON to a medium saucepan over medium heat and cook until it starts to brown. Stir in the onion and garlic and cook until they are soft and fragrant. Add in the remaining ingredients, topping off the mixture with about 4 cups of the broth and seasoning everything with the salt and pepper. Cover the pot and simmer for about 2 hours, stirring occasionally and adding more of the broth as needed, until the beans are quite soft and have absorbed most of the broth. Remove the bay leaf and serve warm.

Braavosi Mussels

MAKES: *4 servings*
COOKING: *20 minutes*
PAIRS WELL WITH: *crusty bread for dipping; creamy pasta;*
Dothraki Blood Pies (page 143); Dōnor Vīgilla (page 219)

When the slaves who founded Braavos first arrived in the mist-shrouded lagoons in the north of Essos, they came with only the rags on their backs and whatever goods were on the ships they had seized. But as they slowly built their tiny colony into the wealthiest and most powerful of the Free Cities that we know today, it was their lagoon that provided all the sustenance they needed. And chief among that was shellfish.

It is no wonder, then, that the Braavosi love of seafood endures today. Within the city you'll find everything from street urchins crying the day's catch to the more subtle offerings of the finest chefs in the city. This recipe hails from one of the more respectable of the dock-side regions, where the taverns offer large portions of mussels to willing patrons. The bulk of preparation goes into making the sauce, as the mussels themselves steam in a matter of minutes. Tinged red and just a touch spicy, the sauce complements the mussels beautifully and is perfect with a side of toasted bread for dipping.

3 tablespoons olive oil
4 garlic cloves, minced
½ yellow onion, diced
1 tablespoon red curry paste
1 tablespoon honey
½ cup chicken broth
1 cup white wine

1 bay leaf
½ teaspoon Aleppo pepper flakes
½ teaspoon ground sumac
1 tablespoon red or white wine vinegar
Salt and ground black pepper
2 pounds mussels
2 tablespoons unsalted butter

➤ HEAT THE OIL in a large pot. Add the garlic and onion, cooking for several minutes until the mixture is fragrant and the onion has softened. Stir in the curry paste and honey and cook for another minute. Pour in the broth and white wine, along with the bay leaf, Aleppo pepper, sumac, and vinegar, then season with the salt and pepper. Cook for about 5 minutes, then add the mussels and cover the pot. Cook for another 6 to 7 minutes, until all the mussels have popped open. Discard any that do not open.

➤ TRANSFER THE MUSSELS with a slotted spoon to a medium bowl and cover to keep warm. Stir the butter into the sauce and cook for a couple of minutes, until the sauce thickens somewhat. Pour the sauce over the mussels and serve straightaway with lightly toasted bread to sop up the sauce.

MAESTER'S NOTE *Some folk like to stir in a dollop of coconut milk or goat cheese in place of the butter for a creamier sauce, and it's a variation I've found well worth trying.*

Dornish Roasted Red Pepper Paste

MAKES: *1 batch*
PREP: *5 minutes*
PAIRS WELL WITH: *olives; feta; Flaky Flatbread (page 122);*
Dōnor Vīgilla (page 219)

his next dish is native to the Red Mountains, which separate Dorne from both the Reach and the stormlands and are famous for their impassible heights and windswept crags. It may surprise those who have never traveled there to know that the Red Mountains are home to spots of sheer loveliness as well, such as the high pastures and meadows above Yronwood. It was there, among the Yronwood family, that I first sampled this incomparable dish in a lavish feast in the family gardens, which overlook the Boneway and river below.

Here, roasted red peppers are blended into a smooth paste with a vivid color. This dish makes for an excellent addition to a sideboard buffet, served alongside cheeses, flatbreads, and spice-cured olives. The flavor of the walnuts is barely perceptible, but nonetheless lends the dish an earthiness and texture that it would otherwise lack. Roasting the red peppers adds a touch of sweetness alongside the molasses, while a little zip of lemon brightens it all. This paste can be served slightly warmed in the evening with a drizzle of olive oil, but it is generally enjoyed cold during midday meals.

6 to 8 ounces roasted red peppers
2 to 4 tablespoons olive oil, as needed
¼ cup walnuts
1 garlic clove, minced
2 tablespoons red curry paste

½ cup bread crumbs
2 tablespoons pomegranate molasses
½ teaspoon Aleppo pepper flakes
1 teaspoon ground sumac

➤ COMBINE ALL THE INGREDIENTS in a food processor and pulse until you have an even paste, adding a little extra olive oil as needed to reach a spreadable consistency. The mixture will keep, covered, for several days in the fridge.

CHELSEA'S NOTE *Jarred peppers work well in this recipe, but to roast your own red peppers, preheat the oven to 425°F. Brush two red bell peppers (deseeded and sliced in half) with olive oil and roast for 20 to 30 minutes, until soft and slightly charred. Allow the peppers to cool slightly for a few minutes, then peel. Continue with the recipe as written above.*

Salted Cod Cakes

MAKES: *About 10 cakes*
SOAKING: *24 hours*
PREP: *5 minutes*
COOKING: *20 minutes*
PAIRS WELL WITH: *beer; Ironborn Ship's Biscuits (page 136);*
Garlic Broth with Chunks of Whitefish, Carrot, and Onion (page 106)

Preserved meat and fish, including salt cod, salt pork, salt beef, and salt mutton, are essential winter fare in much of the North. Nevertheless, salt cod also has culinary merits that make it a worthy addition to any larder even in more hospitable seasons. The common complaint from those unfamiliar with how best to cook with salt cod—of which I was one myself until recently—is that the salt flavor is too overpowering for it to be anything other than survival fare. This doesn't have to be the case. In the right recipe, salt cod can be a delicacy. I first encountered the fishcakes described below at a tavern in Maidenpool. I was seduced by the little morsels quite against my will when, intending to enjoy just one or two, I quickly requested another serving, as well as the recipe from their cook.

Versions of these fishcakes can be found up and down the eastern coast of Westeros, from Eastwatch-by-the-Sea to Storm's End. The black brothers often make do with whatever dried beans they have stored for winter, but farther south, chickpeas are preferred. These legumes give the cakes much-needed body and substance while balancing out that inherent saltiness. Just a touch of herbs complements and elevates the cod, making an eminently satisfying dish for such a simple recipe.

½ pound salt cod
One 15-ounce can chickpeas, drained
 and rinsed
¼ teaspoon dried thyme

¼ teaspoon fennel seeds
1 egg
1 cup bread crumbs
Lemon, for serving

➤ **BEFORE BEGINNING THE RECIPE,** break the salt cod up into bite-sized pieces and soak in a bowl of cool water in the fridge for about 24 hours. Change out the water every 4 hours to keep the cakes from getting too salty.

➤ **COMBINE THE SOAKED COD,** chickpeas, herbs, and egg in a food processor and pulse until no large pieces remain. Transfer to a medium bowl and stir in the bread crumbs until you have a nice firm mixture that holds its shape. Using your hands, form this mixture into patties about 3 inches across and ½ inch thick.

➤ **HEAT SOME VEGETABLE OIL** in a large frying pan set over medium heat. Working in batches, cook a few of the cod cakes for a minute or two on each side, until somewhat crisped and a dark golden brown. Remove to a separate plate while you cook the next batch. Enjoy warm with a squeeze of fresh lemon, when available.

Potted Hare

MAKES: *About 4 servings*
PREP: *10 minutes*
COOKING: *1½ hours*
PAIRS WELL WITH: *white wine; crusty bread; Redwyne Roasted Grapes (page 68)*

omestic hares are given over to the care of skilled warreners, who raise them in huge earthworks riddled with burrows, while wild hares flourish amongst the royal forests and rolling hills between the riverlands and the Vale. Although trapping hares is the most efficient method for harvesting them, many young highborn lads enjoy hunting hares with hounds. The pelts of these creatures provide luxuriously soft fur for trimming clothing, while their lean meat is prized for its flavor.

This dish is my favorite way to preserve meat, save for submerging a roast in honey until needed. In the months of late autumn, potted hare is an incomparable addition to any sideboard. The meat is stewed until soft with wine and herbs, then shredded and packed into clay vessels. A layer of clarified butter is poured over the top, which acts as an effective lid, capping the meat and containing the liquid. When scooped out again, the meat is soft and spreadable, and I quite enjoy it atop a piece of crusty bread.

1 pound rabbit meat or boneless chicken thighs
1 cup white wine
3 uncooked bacon strips, diced
1 tablespoon minced fresh sage
1 teaspoon coriander seeds

Pinch of ground black pepper
Pinch of ground cinnamon
Pinch of ground nutmeg
2 tablespoons dried currants (optional)
1 to 2 sticks unsalted butter

recipe continues

- **In a large pot**, combine all the ingredients except the butter with 2 cups of water and set over medium heat. Once the mix is simmering, cook for 1 hour, topping up with additional water as needed to keep the meat mostly submerged. Flip the meat occasionally to ensure even cooking.
- **After the first hour**, use a slotted spoon to transfer the meat to a medium bowl and shred it with two forks until no large pieces remain. Return the shredded meat to the pot and cook for another 15 minutes or so, until the meat has absorbed some of the broth.
- **Remove the pot** from the heat and transfer the meat to several wide-mouthed jars. Press the meat down firmly to pack it into the jars, then spoon a little of the broth over the top to fill in any cracks, leaving at least a ½ inch of space at the top of the jars. Allow the jars to cool somewhat while you clarify the butter.
- **To clarify the butter**, melt it in a small saucepan over medium-low heat. Continue to cook for several minutes until the butter turns white and foamy on top, then reduce the heat to low. The white foam will gradually subside, then sink to the bottom of the pan. At that point, remove the butter from the heat and strain it through cheesecloth or a coffee filter into a clean container.
- **Pour just enough** of the clarified butter over the potted hare to cover it by about ¼ inch, reserving the remaining butter in the fridge for other purposes. Chill the potted meat for up to a week, and bring to room temperature to enjoy.

Riverlands Creamed Leeks

MAKES: *2 to 4 servings*
PREP: *5 minutes*
COOKING: *15 minutes*
PAIRS WELL WITH: *fish or poultry dishes*

Some of the most productive agricultural land in all of Westeros can be found in the river-lands, although only particular crops are suited to the rich sandy soil there. Along the Red Fork in particular, which takes its name from the ruddy hue of its deep muddy banks, row upon row of leeks can be found growing from spring to early autumn. Riverland leeks are prized by highborn and smallfolk alike for their flavor and are used in a wide variety of soups and side dishes. Leeks, like other alliums, are widely supposed by the Citadel to have considerable health benefits, in addition to culinary merits.

One absolutely winning dish I was fortunate enough to try when last passing through the riverlands was a simple yet eminently satisfying side of leeks stewed in almond milk. The Tully cook—Raymund, I believe was his name—was good enough to share his recipe. It turns out that blanching the leeks before stewing them in the almond milk leaches away their sharpness, leaving only the much mellowed sweetness of the vegetable itself. The leeks retain a residual crunch as a counterpoint to the creaminess of the sauce, and the pinch of saffron gives the whole dish a rich golden color.

1 cup almond milk, store-bought or
   homemade (page 44), warmed
1 tablespoon rice flour or bread crumbs
Pinch of saffron threads

2 leeks, cleaned and cut into ½-inch slices
1 tablespoon honey
Pinch of salt
Freshly ground white pepper

➤ IN A SMALL BOWL, combine the almond milk, rice flour, and saffron. Set aside.

➤ BRING A MEDIUM POT of water to a boil. Add the leeks and cook for about 5 minutes. Drain them and transfer to a large frying pan over medium heat. Add the almond milk mixture, honey, and salt. Stir for 5 to 10 minutes, until the liquid has thickened and coats the leeks. Remove the pan from the heat and sprinkle a little of the pepper on top of everything before serving.

Soups & Stews

Soups and stews are popular at all levels of society throughout Westeros. In part, this is due to practical reasons: The poor—those with limited access to ingredients, especially meat—can rely on soups and stews to stretch their supplies and feed a large number of people economically. The highborn enjoy soup as a course in a large feast, a dish to whet the appetite for the main course yet to come. Soups also offer ways to revive ingredients that have been put by for the long winter, and to scrounge yet one more meal out of ingredients that would elsewise be considered scrap. Of equal importance, a stew can be kept cooking for days. There are even stories that some of the pot shops of King's Landing have had the same cauldron of stew cooking for an entire generation. It's a way to keep food fresh and a hot meal ready to be served at any time, ideal for the many inns and taverns throughout the realm.

Pottage
with Spring Greens

MAKES: *4 servings*
PREP: *5 minutes*
COOKING: *20 minutes*
PAIRS WELL WITH: *bread, such as Jaedo Havon (page 128);*
creamy cheese; white wine

Early spring is a perilous time in Westeros. The snows are melting and the world is becoming green, but most new crops have only just been planted and are not close to ready for harvest yet. In the Vale and elsewhere across the realm, the smallfolk call this period the hunger gap, when the winter stores have often run very low, and there is little new forage to be found. It is in this season that fresh greens, often little more than weeds, are so crucial.

This pottage makes good use of such greenery, blending it into a dish that falls somewhere between a porridge and a soup. Thick and hearty, with a slight greenish tint from the leaves, it nourishes and sustains without feeling as heavy as some winter dishes. The oatmeal and leek flavors are the strongest, chased with a hint of whatever the foraged greens bring to the dish. Nutmeg and a bit of pepper, if you have them, round out the other flavors.

2 tablespoons unsalted butter
¼ cup rolled oats
2 leeks, white parts only, washed and
* roughly chopped*
2½ cups chicken or vegetable broth

1 cup loosely packed greens, roughly chopped
* (see Maester's Notes)*
Pinch of ground nutmeg
Salt and ground black pepper

➤ IN A MEDIUM SAUCEPAN, melt the butter over medium heat. Stir in the oats and cook for several minutes, until they start to turn golden brown. Add the leeks and stir to coat in butter. Cook for about 5 minutes or so, until the leeks are soft. Add the broth and return to a simmer. Cook for another 10 minutes or so, then stir in the greens. After another minute, remove the pottage from the heat and season with the nutmeg, salt, and pepper. At this point, you can either serve as is or puree the pottage with an immersion blender.

MAESTER'S NOTES *Some of the first spring greens to sprout include nettle, wild garlic, lamb's-quarters, violets, sorrel, spinach, and even hops and asparagus. The recipe is versatile and adaptable, based on what you can find.*

If you wish for a more elegant version of the soup, replace ¹/₂ cup of the broth with 1 cup almond milk or cow's milk. Cook as instructed, blend, then pass through a sieve for a smoother consistency.

Meereenese Soup

with Ginger

MAKES: *4 servings*
PREP: *5 minutes*
COOKING: *15 minutes*
PAIRS WELL WITH: *Flaky Flatbread (page 122);*
Stewed Plums (page 175)

I found this to be one of the more tame culinary offerings to come out of Meereen—a city whose myriad recipes for preparing dog do not appeal to most travelers from Westeros. Although it's one of the more costly spices in Westeros, ginger flourishes easily in the tropical climate of Essos. As a consequence, it is almost commonplace in the cuisine there, enjoyed by most levels of society, from pit fighters to princes. This particular recipe is said to have considerable health benefits, and some among Meereen's warrior class insist that it also enhances the strength and bravery of those who consume it regularly. As a result, ginger soup is a popular dish among the free companies who sell their swords, as well as the nobility of Essos.

The vibrant golden color of this broth makes a striking first impression, followed closely by its tantalizing aroma of spice. The addition of ground almonds gives the broth a little extra body, punctuated by sweet, savory, and acidic ingredients all competing for dominance. Cooks in wealthier households often add some shredded chicken meat to the broth and garnish with a smattering of rose petals and pomegranate seeds for a showy presentation.

1 tablespoon olive oil
1 shallot, sliced thin
2 teaspoons freshly grated ginger
2 teaspoons Old Ghis Spice Blend
   (page 25)
¼ cup ground almonds

2 tablespoons jaggery or brown sugar
1 tablespoon lemon juice
4 cups chicken broth
Organic rose petals, to garnish (optional)
Pomegranate seeds, to garnish (optional)

➤➤ POUR THE OLIVE OIL into the bottom of a medium saucepot and set over medium heat. Add the shallot and cook for several minutes, until soft. Stir in the ginger and spice blend for about a minute, then add the almonds, sugar, and lemon juice. Add the chicken broth and bring to a simmer. Serve hot as is, or puree with an immersion blender for a smoother texture. If desired, garnish with rose petals or pomegranate seeds.

Onion Broth
with Carrot and Goat

MAKES: *5 to 6 servings*
PREP: *15 minutes*
COOKING: *1 hour*
PAIRS WELL WITH: *Fried Breadsticks (page 123); ale; mead*

Broths such as this are common in the North, especially on the Wall, where even with the generosity of the Starks of Winterfell, the storehouses of the Night's Watch can run thin in the months of late winter. I had the pleasure of touring these storehouses at the end of autumn one year and saw the prodigious supply of food laid by: all manner of dried fruits, ropes of sausages too numerous to count, barrels of dried beans and grains, entire rooms of game meat frozen solid by the cold of the ice. Such a supply is perhaps one advantage of living on Westeros's northernmost edge, although a harsh bargain elsewise, to be sure. The head steward assured me, however, that the food would be scarcely enough to last the men if the winter proved long. When the stores begin to stretch thin, the thick stews of autumn and early winter are replaced by broths with fewer ingredients to fill them. Nonetheless, the clever cooks do what they can to enliven such meals with the use of herbs and spices, as well as what vegetables and meats they can spare.

The onion broth recorded here is one such concoction. Ale, goat, and carrots give extra flavor to the body of the soup, which doesn't require significant quantities of ingredients. I must say, however, that I think this recipe has significant merits apart from its practical value of stretching ingredients. The salt pork and herbs impart flavor that is rich enough for a first course at a feast, and the soup is satisfying enough to be a midday meal if served with crusty bread and hard cheese.

2 small sprigs sage
2 small sprigs mint
4 ounces salt pork
5 cups water
1 cup dark beer or ale

1 yellow onion, roughly chopped
Pinch of Stag's Spice (page 25)
1 cup carrots, chopped small
8 ounces ground goat meat
1 to 2 tablespoons bacon fat or olive oil

➤ BIND THE SAGE AND mint together with some kitchen twine, then combine the salt pork, water, ale, bundle of herbs, and onion in a large pot. Set over medium heat and simmer for 45 minutes. Remove the bundle of herbs, season the broth with the Stag's Spice, and add the carrots.

➤ WHILE THE BROTH IS simmering, set a skillet over medium heat and brown the goat meat in the bacon fat before adding it to the broth pot. Let everything simmer together for 15 minutes, until the carrots are tender. Skim some of the fat off the top of the broth if you like, then serve hot.

MAESTER'S NOTES *For a tidier soup, strain the broth into a clean pot after the initial simmer of 45 minutes, reserving some of the onions if you would like to add them back in. Return the pot to the heat and continue with the recipe as written with the addition of the Stag's Spice and carrots.*

If salt pork and goat are difficult to come by, bacon and lamb meat, respectively, may be substituted.

Dragonstone Jaerhilla

MAKES: *4 to 6 servings*
PREP: *15 minutes*
COOKING: *3 hours*
PAIRS WELL WITH: *Jaedo Havon (page 128);*
black rice; Myrish Firewine (page 210)

The dragons of old, and some say their riders as well, thrived on heat: hot weather, hot food, hot baths. For this reason, Dragonstone made an ideal foothold for the Targaryens in Westeros. I have not been to the island myself, but it is said that the cellars of the castle are connected to a vast warren of tunnels and rooms that grow warmer the deeper they descend. Indeed, feral dragons were once known to make their homes in the smoking caves of the Dragonmont because of the intensity of the heat deep within. These peculiar properties of Dragonstone led to the creation of one of the most exciting recipes in this collection. It seems that there was a room, or perhaps several, in the bowels of the castle's keep where dragon eggs were stored, warmed by the volcanic core of the island. Some enterprising cook worked out that the heat there could also be used to slowly cook food, such as this spiced goat stew. It was in the hot darkness of those tunnels that the first iteration of the stew was born.

An approximation of this unique dish can be created by slow cooking the meat until it becomes incredibly tender and using a seasoning blend from Essos to ensure each bite bursts with flavor. Although not as fiery as many Dornish dishes, this stew's spice profile has a steady warming effect that will please most palates. Stewing renders the goat meat (which is often quite tough when roasted) soft and tender. The meat takes on the rich flavors of the cooking broth, which can be further thickened for a more stew-like consistency. This dish pairs especially well with the summer loaf Jaedo Havon, and is perfection itself when chased by a nip of Myrish Firewine.

2 tablespoons olive oil
1 yellow onion, sliced
2 garlic cloves, minced
2 pounds goat, lamb, or mutton meat, cubed
1 tablespoon red curry paste

2 tablespoons Freehold Spice Blend
 (page 24)
1 teaspoon salt
Water, to cover
3 heaping tablespoons diced dried apricots

recipe continues

➤ PREHEAT THE OVEN to 300°F and set aside a large casserole or ovenproof dish.

➤ IN A LARGE FRYING PAN, heat the olive oil over medium-high heat. Add the onion and garlic and cook for several minutes, until soft and fragrant. Add the cubed meat and cook for another few minutes, until browned on all sides. Stir in the red curry paste, spice blend, and salt. Transfer everything to the casserole dish, and add just enough water to cover by an inch. Cover the dish with a lid or aluminum foil and cook for about 2½ hours, then add the apricots and cook for another 30 minutes, until the meat is tender and the fruit has started to fall apart. Serve warm.

MAESTER'S NOTE *If you would like to thicken the broth once the meat has finished cooking, strain out the meat and apricots using a sieve and keep them warm in a separate bowl. In a large frying pan, melt 1 tablespoon unsalted butter over medium heat. Stir in 1 tablespoon all-purpose flour for about a minute, until golden, then gradually stir in the hot broth from the casserole dish. The whole mixture should thicken, at which point the meat may be added back in and reheated, along with the apricots.*

Spicy Lentil Stew

MAKES: *About 4 servings*
PREP: *10 minutes*
COOKING: *50 minutes*
PAIRS WELL WITH: *Flaky Flatbread (page 122);*
hard cheeses

There is very little that the sands of Dorne have in common with the windy reaches of the Vale of Arryn, but versions of this lentil stew are common in both regions. When I was a young man at the Citadel, an older novice named Roymar Stone first introduced me to this dish in order to disabuse me of my notion that a particular soup served once a fortnight in our hall was "quite good." He insisted that if he made us a pot of "Snakewood Broil," a real lentil and lamb stew, I would recant—and I did. Imagine my surprise when I next encountered the same dish over a decade later in the northern reaches of Dorne, where the stew is not only common but considered to be a unique regional delicacy.

This spicy broth, fortified by either lamb or goat meat, is a hearty meal in any clime. It is full-bodied, peppery, and savory enough to please any palate, whether humble or highborn. Although the Dornish version is typically a little more heavy-handed with the hot pepper, that particular ingredient is easily proportioned to the tastes of the cook in question. Whether from Dorne or the Vale, this stew pairs well with hard cheese and flatbread.

2 spicy sausages, such as chorizo, roughly
  chopped
1 to 2 tablespoons olive oil
½ yellow onion, diced
1 garlic clove, minced
1 small eggplant, peeled and cubed
8 ounces ground lamb or goat meat
¼ cup molasses

1 cup dried lentils, of any color
½ teaspoon smoked paprika
½ teaspoon ground cumin
1 teaspoon salt
Pinch of cinnamon
Dried pepper flakes, to taste
4 cups beef broth

➤ IN A LARGE SAUCEPAN, sear the sausages for several minutes until their juices run and the meat is cooked through, then transfer the sausages to a separate bowl, leaving the sausage oils in the pan. Add the olive oil to the pan, then cook the onion, garlic, and eggplant in the oils until soft and golden, about 5 minutes. Add the remaining ingredients, along with the cooked sausage, and allow the stew to simmer for around 40 minutes, until the meat is soft.

Creamy Chestnut Soup

MAKES: *2 to 4 servings*
PREP: *5 minutes*
COOKING: *30 minutes*
PAIRS WELL WITH: *Fried Breadsticks (page 123);*
sliced apples and cheddar cheese; white wine or mead

Chestnut trees thrive in nearly every part of Westeros and are especially prized by the smallfolk, who gather the fallen nuts even from forests where they have no leave to hunt. Most lords will hang a poacher if they catch one, but few if any will deny their people the sweepings of the forest floor. In Maidenpool, there is even a children's rhyme: "Oh tell me, tell me, where do the red nuts fall? They'll take your head for a buck, or a hand if you've luck, but never for a nut to old Harrenhal."

That's not to say that chestnuts aren't also well-loved by those who dwell in the great cities of the Seven Kingdoms. Every autumn in King's Landing, at the height of harvest, chestnuts are roasted atop braziers in the streets and artfully arrayed on steaming platters for those with a little extra coin. The scent of those roasting nuts hangs in the air, giving the city a festive feel before the winter sets in. In the Red Keep, this sweet harvest is incorporated into stuffings, breads, pastries, and soups, such as the one below. Thick and creamy, this favorite of King Robert also incorporates chickpeas, which enhance the texture and bring out subtler shades of flavor from the chestnuts. Topped with a swirl of cream and a pinch of nutmeg, this soup is only a distant relative of the stews common in villages and holdfasts.

1 tablespoon unsalted butter
1 to 2 shallots, peeled and sliced thin
Splash of Cognac or brandy
2½ cups chicken broth
8 ounces cooked chestnuts
  (see Chelsea's Note)

One 15-ounce can chickpeas, drained
  and rinsed
Pinch of ground nutmeg, plus more to garnish
1 cup milk, warmed
1 to 2 tablespoons heavy cream, to garnish

➤ MELT THE BUTTER in the bottom of a medium saucepan over medium heat. Add the shallots and cook for several minutes, until soft and fragrant. Add the Cognac and stir for another minute or so. Add the broth, chestnuts, chickpeas, and nutmeg. Reduce the heat to medium-low and cook for about 30 minutes. Puree the mixture with an immersion blender, adding in the milk until you reach your desired consistency. Transfer the soup to serving bowls, garnish with a swirl of the heavy cream and a sprinkle of nutmeg, and serve warm.

CHELSEA'S NOTE *Prepackaged cooked chestnuts work well in this recipe, but to roast your own chestnuts, preheat the oven to 425°F and bring a medium pot of water to boil. Using a sharp knife and a great deal of care, carve an X into the flat side of each chestnut, then lower them into the water and boil for 30 seconds. Drain the nuts and move them to an ovenproof pan to roast in the oven for 25 to 30 minutes, until they have begun to split open. Allow the chestnuts to cool until they can be handled, then carefully peel away their hard outer shells and the papery layers inside. They can be enjoyed as is, or used for other recipes such as the soup.*

Egg-Lemon Soup

MAKES: *4 to 6 servings*
PREP: *5 minutes*
COOKING: *20 minutes*
PAIRS WELL WITH: *flatbread; feta; hard-boiled eggs; Dōnor Vīgilla (page 219)*

*L*emons might be costly in other parts of Westeros, but in Dorne and parts of Essos they are so plentiful that at the height of the season cooks and smallfolk must find innovative ways to make use of each heavy harvest. Lemons are used to flavor fish and meat, incorporated into desserts, dried whole by the thousands, and still there is fruit left over for use in creative and unique recipes. This soup is one such innovation, and rarely have I encountered a soup that has such a cheerful disposition.

At least half the time in our Seven Kingdoms, soups are a way to stretch supplies that are running low, or to revitalize ingredients that have been preserved for long winters. Not so with this recipe. Beaten eggs thicken the soup to a silky texture that bursts with lemony brightness. Tender pasta floats in the thick, creamy broth along with bits of roasted chicken meat, as I suggest in my notes below. Shredded carrots and thinly sliced shallots top each bowl with a splash of color and crunch. It is a soup that is warm, sunny, and good—just like the place it comes from.

2 tablespoons olive oil	Zest of 1 lemon
2 shallots, sliced thin	Juice of 1 lemon
½ cup finely chopped carrots	2 eggs
5 cups chicken broth	Salt and ground black pepper
¾ cup orzo	Fresh parsley, to garnish

➤ IN A SMALL SAUCEPAN, warm the olive oil over medium heat. Add the shallots and carrots and cook until the carrots are soft, about 5 minutes, stirring every so often so the shallots don't burn. Remove from the heat and set aside.

➤ IN A MEDIUM POT, bring the broth to a boil, then reduce the heat slightly and add the orzo. Let the broth and orzo simmer until the pasta is cooked through but not too soft, around 8 minutes. While the orzo is cooking, whisk together the lemon zest, lemon juice, and eggs in a separate bowl until smooth. Begin whisking the egg mixture again furiously, and once the orzo has finished cooking, slowly pour a ladle of the hot broth into the egg mixture to cook the eggs without scrambling them. Pour the hot egg mixture back into the pot with the broth and pasta, whisking for approximately 30 seconds to combine. Remove from the heat and season with salt and pepper.

➤ LADLE THE SOUP into serving bowls, then heap the cooked carrots and shallots on top. Sprinkle with a little parsley for color. This soup can be served warm or cold.

MAESTER'S NOTE *I found a similar soup being served when I visited Pentos recently, but with lime juice and lime zest in place of the lemon, and cooked rice in place of the orzo. They also added a pinch of ground sumac, which is slightly lemony on its own, but with earthy undertones that meld well with the other, simpler flavors in the soup. Cooked, shredded chicken can also be added to either version of the soup to turn this dish into a more robust meal.*

Garlic Broth

with Chunks of Whitefish, Carrot, and Onion

MAKES: *2 to 4 servings*
PREP: *15 minutes*
COOKING: *45 minutes*
PAIRS WELL WITH: *Ironborn Ship's Biscuits (page 136);*
Salted Cod Cakes (page 82); tangy goat cheese

Known as much for its medicinal qualities as for its flavor in the kitchen, garlic broth is valued by royal chefs and rustics alike. Every maester who has forged a silver link is aware of its ability to expunge ill humors and drive the cold from a body. I must also confess a certain personal affection for this concoction, held ever since a spring visit to the stormlands in my youth. I took a chill on Cape Wrath, and without the ministrations of a certain ship's cook and the healing properties of this soup, I am not certain that I would be here now to record these recipes.

Through boiling, the harsh bite of the garlic—which is so valued in hot poultices—is rendered more mellow, almost buttery. It lends this nourishing broth a feeling of creaminess without the need for fresh cream. The small bites of whitefish provide a little texture alongside the carrots. Overall, it is a subtly enticing soup, perfect for those who are recovering from a variety of ailments and afflictions, as well as those seeking simply to warm themselves on a cold winter's day.

2 garlic heads, peeled
4 cups water
2 cups chicken stock
Pinch of ground black pepper
Pinch of ground cloves

Pinch of salt
8 ounces whitefish (such as cod, grouper,
*   or halibut), cut into chunks*
2 carrots, chopped
½ cup pearl onions

➤ COMBINE THE GARLIC, water, stock, pepper, cloves, and salt in a medium saucepan over medium-high heat. Bring to a boil, then lower the heat slightly and simmer for about 30 minutes, until the garlic is very soft. Mash the garlic with a spoon and add the remaining ingredients. Simmer for another 10 to 15 minutes, until the carrots are soft. Serve hot.

MAESTER'S NOTE *If you prefer, you can also chop the heads of garlic in half before putting them into the water for the initial boil, skins and all. Simply strain out the garlic and its skins after this first boil, then return the broth to the pot. This method is especially effective if you are simply making the broth, and can discard the rest. The base broth can be adapted to taste with additional ingredients such as seaweed or other greens, a variety of root vegetables, and other fish, both fresh and smoked.*

Beef and Barley Soup

MAKES: *4 servings*
PREP: *15 minutes*
COOKING: *About 2 hours*
PAIRS WELL WITH: *sharp cheese; Sigil Bread (page 113);*
Apple Crisps (page 176)

ariations of this soup can be found across much of Westeros, but it is most commonly found north of the Neck. Although different regions employ their own subtly different takes on the recipe, the essential formula is the same: stewed beef, barley cooked soft, and an assortment of root vegetables. The majority of the ingredients can be dried or preserved during the harvest season, making this soup a staple during the long winters.

Despite the fact that versions of this dish are served throughout the Seven Kingdoms, I could find no written recipe in my research. However, this is not surprising, as the soup is consumed primarily by smallfolk, and only in the North is it sometimes served in lordly halls. This is the bane of archivists: the most mundane details are often lost to history, while the wedding feasts between great houses are recorded for all time. For that reason alone this recipe was worth including, inspired as it was by similar soups I was served in several different cottages.

3 tablespoons unsalted butter

1 pound beef stew meat, cut into bite-size pieces

4 ounces sliced mushrooms

½ cup diced turnips

1 to 2 carrots, sliced small, greens reserved

12 pearl onions, peeled

3 garlic cloves, minced

2 tablespoons all-purpose flour

¾ cup pearl barley

1 cup brown ale or red wine

2 cups beef broth

1 to 2 cups water

1 teaspoon fresh or dried thyme

Salt and ground black pepper

➤ MELT THE BUTTER in a medium saucepan over medium heat. Add the meat and brown it on all sides, then remove the meat and set it aside. Add the sliced mushrooms to the same pan and cook for several minutes, until soft. Add the remaining vegetables and garlic and cook for another 5 minutes or so, until the vegetables have started to soften. Sprinkle in the flour and stir until it has been absorbed by the butter. Add the browned meat back into the pot along with the pearl barley, ale, broth, 1 cup water, and thyme.

➤ BRING THE MIXTURE to a simmer and cook for about 1½ hours, until the barley has cooked through and has a soft, chewy texture, topping up with additional water if needed.

➤ MINCE THE RESERVED CARROT GREENS and stir into the stew, then season with the salt and pepper and serve hot.

BREADS

Bread might be the single most common food in our Seven Kingdoms. Bread is an easy, quick, and convenient way to convey nutrition and store resources, and it can be carried to fieldhands as easily as it can be served at a high table. Even two- or three-day-old bread can be used in recipes, while the poor have developed breads intended to be eaten weeks—or, in some cases, as long as a month—after they're baked. Breads produced in castle kitchens, by contrast, are usually best enjoyed within a few hours of emerging from the oven. Whether fried on a griddle, baked in an oven, toasted, or enjoyed in a "tear and share" manner, bread has always been one of the foods around which people have gathered. It's there for breakfast, slathered with butter and honey; it's dipped into stew at midday; and it's used to sop up every last morsel of a flavorful dinner.

Sigil Bread

MAKES: *About 8 to 10 shapes*
PREP: *About 30 minutes*
BAKING: *20 minutes*
PAIRS WELL WITH: *soups and stews, such as Beef and Barley Soup (page 108);
fresh butter and honey or jam*

Some archival records indicate that small breads formed and baked into special shapes might be one of the few traditions from the age of the First Men who survived the coming of the Andals. According to some scholars, these shaped breads were likely intended for some ritualistic purpose rather than for eating. Nonetheless, the basic idea has remained essentially the same, evolving over the centuries into the edible bread we enjoy now. Different regions have their own varieties, though in the noble houses, the breads typically take the form of the House's sigil.

Formed in an endless variety of fanciful shapes, these breads make for a memorable plating. Created from a coarser flour so that each small loaf holds its shape and details better, the bread's texture is firm and dense, and the flavor both simple and satisfying.

5 cups coarse whole wheat flour
1 teaspoon baking soda
Pinch of salt
*6 tablespoons unsalted butter, room
   temperature*

¼ cup honey
2 eggs
About 2 cups buttermilk or sour milk

➤ PREHEAT THE OVEN to 350°F.

➤ IN A LARGE MIXING BOWL, combine the dry ingredients, then rub in the butter until you have a mixture that resembles bread crumbs. Stir in the honey and one of the eggs, followed by just enough of the buttermilk to reach a soft, workable dough. On a lightly floured surface, roll the dough out until it is around ½ inch thick, then carefully cut it into your desired shapes with a sharp knife. Give the shapes a few decorative scores, then transfer them to a baking sheet lined with parchment paper. In a small bowl, beat the remaining egg with a little water, then brush the tops of the shapes all over with the egg wash.

➤ BAKE FOR AROUND 20 MINUTES, until a lovely golden brown.

Sesame Rings

MAKES: *8 rings*
PREP: *30 minutes*
RISING: *1 hour 20 minutes*
BAKING: *15 minutes*
PAIRS WELL WITH: *jams and honey; feta cheese;*
Mustard from Oldtown (page 21)

Archival records indicate that these rings, although a common enough street food now, date back at least to Aegon I Targaryen's arrival in King's Landing. As such, it is unclear whether they were introduced by the Targaryen monarchs after the Conquest, or adopted by them upon arrival like so many other customs. In any case, these versatile sesame rounds are seldom found outside of King's Landing and its surrounding countryside, making them something of a culinary oddity.

The rings are baked by the hundreds in the ovens of King's Landing, releasing a smell of toasted sesame seeds that wafts through the predawn gloom of twisted streets. Once baked, the still-warm bread is stacked into baskets for vendors to carefully shoulder and peddle through the streets. Some enterprising bakers have been known to experiment with a variety of seeds other than sesame, although their efforts have been met with middling response; the sesame variant is by far the most popular. With a slightly crisp exterior covered with nutty seeds, and a dense, chewy inside, it is no wonder the original recipe remains a beloved classic. Many enjoy the rings plain, straight from the oven, but in finer households they are often enjoyed with a bit of honey or jam.

4 cups all-purpose flour, plus more as needed
1 tablespoon sugar
1 teaspoon salt
1½ cups warm water
¼ cup olive or sesame oil
2 teaspoons instant dry yeast

TOPPING
¼ cup grape molasses
¼ cup water
2 tablespoons all-purpose flour
1½ cups sesame seeds, toasted

➤ **IN A LARGE MIXING BOWL,** combine the flour, sugar, and salt. In a smaller bowl, combine the warm water, oil, and yeast, allowing the mixture to stand for a minute or two until the yeast has started to bubble. Pour the yeast mixture into the middle of the flour mixture, then mix everything together using a spoon or your hands. Continue mixing, adding a little more flour if needed, until the dough is no longer too sticky to handle.

➤ **TURN THE DOUGH OUT** onto a lightly floured surface and knead for around 5 minutes, until the dough bounces back when poked. Lightly grease a large bowl, then place the dough in the bowl and cover with plastic wrap or a damp towel. Allow the dough to rise somewhere warm for at least 1 hour, or until it has doubled in size.

➤ **WHILE THE DOUGH RISES,** prepare the topping by combining the molasses, water, and flour in a shallow bowl you can use to dip the dough into later. Pour the sesame seeds into a separate shallow bowl. Set both aside.

➤ **ONCE THE DOUGH HAS RISEN,** preheat the oven to 400°F. Punch down the dough, then lightly flour an even work surface and divide the dough into 16 pieces. Gently roll each piece out into a rope about 24 inches long. Place the ropes in pairs, matching them according to length, then twist together the ropes in each pair from one end to the other. Curl the braided rope into a circle and pinch the ends together, then roll the joined ends on the work surface to help them stick even better. Repeat with all the dough until you have eight finished rings.

➤ **WHISK UP THE MOLASSES MIXTURE,** then dip a ring into the liquid, making sure all surfaces of the dough are evenly covered. Transfer the ring to the bowl with the sesame seeds and spoon the seeds over the dough until the ring is fully covered. Move the ring to a baking sheet and repeat with the rest of the rings. Allow the sesame rings to rise again for about 20 to 30 minutes, until they look a bit puffy.

➤ **ONCE ALL THE RINGS** have risen, bake for about 12 to 15 minutes, until a rich golden brown. Allow to cool slightly before enjoying.

Bread and Salt

MAKES: *2 loaves*
PREP: *15 minutes*
RISING: *1 hour*
BAKING: *30 minutes*
PAIRS WELL WITH: *meaty roasts; any ale;*
Winter Town Wassail (page 214)

While the custom of offering guests bread and salt is observed across all of Westeros, you'll find regional twists on the classic recipe that enliven the tradition. Any quantity and quality of bread and salt is sufficient to secure guest right, but extra effort is often put forth for special occasions—especially by the wealthier highborn families for whom first impressions are everything. Those in the Reach often grind colorful blooms into their salt to give it a range of hues, and score the dough to resemble flowers. In the North, hearty loaves made with rye and barley contain salt smoked over applewood. In Dorne, flatbread is quickly baked on hot stones then dipped in pure sea salt kissed with fiery pepper flakes.

This basic recipe is suitable for any region of Westeros and any gathering, be it of friends or rivals. The dough is braided and coiled into a round loaf, yielding small segments that are easy to tear and gently dip into the well of salt at the bread's center. With a slightly crisped crust and soft fluffy interior, the bread is an excellent conveyer of salt to the mouth. It is said that in certain parts of Essos, decorative bread has partially taken root as an appetizer, preferably served with flavored dipping oils or whipped, sweetened butter with spices.

1½ cups milk, warmed

¼ cup (½ stick) unsalted butter, melted

⅓ cup raw sugar

2 teaspoons table salt

1 tablespoon instant dry yeast

5 eggs, 2 left whole for baking into the dough

5 to 6 cups all-purpose flour

1 to 2 tablespoons coarse salt, for dipping

➤ **Combine the milk and butter** in a large mixing bowl. Stir in the sugar, table salt, and yeast until everything has dissolved, about a minute. Beat in two of the eggs, then gradually add in the flour until you have a dough that is no longer sticky and pulls away from the side of the bowl. Turn out the dough onto a lightly floured surface and knead for several minutes, until the dough bounces back when poked. Place the dough in a lightly greased bowl, cover with plastic wrap or a damp towel, and set somewhere warm to rise for about an hour, until doubled in size.

➤ **After the dough has risen,** punch it back down and divide it into six equal portions. On a lightly floured surface, roll each of these portions into a rope about 24 inches long. Braid three of the ropes together, pinching the dough closed at each end of the braid before repeating the process with the remaining three ropes of dough. Coil each braid of dough around itself in a spiral pattern to make a round loaf.

➤ **Preheat the oven** to 350°F and set out a large baking sheet lined with parchment paper. Move the loaves to the baking sheet. Rub the two whole eggs with oil and press one into the center of each loaf. Allow the loaves to rise for 30 minutes or so, until puffy. Finally, beat the remaining egg in a small bowl with a little water and brush it over both loaves. Bake the loaves for about 30 to 40 minutes with the eggs still in the center, until the bread is a rich golden brown. Transfer the baking sheet from the oven and allow the loaves to cool for at least 10 minutes before removing the now-cooked eggs from their centers. Fill the divots from the eggs with the coarse salt or a flavored salt of your choice before serving.

➤ **To serve, allow guests** to tear off pieces of the bread and dip them into the salt.

MAESTER'S NOTE *To better suit regional differences, you can tweak this recipe by swapping some of the flour from all-purpose to rye, whole wheat, oat, etc. Further variety can be achieved by smoking the salt that's served in the center of the bread, adding dried flowers and herbs to it, and so forth. So long as the bread is presented with salt, it will be sufficient for a gesture of hospitality.*

Flaky Flatbread

MAKES: *2 flatbreads*
PREP: *30 minutes*
COOKING: *10 minutes*
RESTING: *10 minutes*
PAIRS WELL WITH: *salty cheese such as feta; cured olives;*
Meereenese Soup with Ginger (page 92)

The forming of these flatbread discs is a complicated but quick process, near to an art form, perfected by the Meereenese bakers for whom this flatbread is a specialty. With a few deft strokes of a rolling pin, the dough is shaped, seasoned, and rolled again before being quickly cooked on a hot griddle. Because the whole process is so fast, Meereen actually has shops that cook the bread on demand, where customers choose their toppings from the day's offerings. Each shop has its own specialty topping, but a common option is salty cheese, honey, and toasted sesame seeds. Other variants include fiery oils, aromatic spice blends, ripe cheeses, and even finely ground meat.

The resulting flatbread features whorls of delicately flaky layers that dissolve on the tongue. Buttery and decadent, this savory disc provides an ideal base for a wide array of toppings and fillings. My favorite combination includes an old Ghiscari spice blend with salty white cheese and a drizzle of honey. The spice renders those same whorls a vibrant yellow color, and each bite bursts with earthy flavors and just a hint of fiery pepper for a long, slow burn.

2 cups all-purpose flour
1 teaspoon salt
1 cup water

8 tablespoons (1 stick) salted butter,
melted and cooled
2 to 3 tablespoons desired fillings (optional)

➤ COMBINE THE FLOUR AND SALT in a medium mixing bowl. Add the water and stir until the dough comes together into a ball. Knead for at least 5 minutes, adding more flour as needed to keep the dough from getting too sticky. Once the dough has a soft and pliable texture, cover the bowl with plastic wrap or a damp towel, and let the dough rest for 10 minutes.

➤ ONCE THE DOUGH HAS RESTED, divide the dough in half. Working with one half at a time, roll out the dough on a generously floured surface until it is no more than ¼ inch thick. Spread 3 tablespoons of the butter and any desired fillings evenly over the top of the dough, then roll the dough up tightly into a long tube. Coil your rolled tube of dough into a spiral like a snail's shell, then dust it with flour and roll it into a flat disc about ½ inch thick. Repeat the process with the remaining dough.

➤ MELT 1 TABLESPOON of the remaining butter in a large skillet over medium heat. Once the pan is hot, add the flatbread and cook for several minutes on each side, until golden brown on both sides. Repeat with the last of the butter and the other flatbread. Allow to cool for a few minutes before serving.

Fried Breadsticks

MAKES: *Several dozen*
PREP: *About 1½ hours*
COOKING: *25 minutes*
PAIRS WELL WITH: *soups or stews, such as Garlic Broth with Chunks of Whitefish, Carrot, and Onion (page 106) or Beef and Barley Soup (page 108); jam or honey*

According to Maester Markwell's insightful tome, "For the Love of Corn: A History of Grain Cultivation in Westeros," both fried dough and dough baked on hot rocks predate bread cooked in ovens by many generations, and the fried dough still popular throughout Westeros is a descendent of the coarse little cakes cooked in quick batches by the First Men over a simple fire. Although hand-ground flour was much coarser than the finely milled wheat of today, I like to think that this dish offers us a small connection to our ancient forebearers.

Fried dough is a staple for many hedge knights and simple folk who live their lives on the move, cooking without the benefit of ovens. This dough is best prepared in a pan or skillet, where it cooks up quite quickly in either butter or bacon grease. Although it is also possible to cook the dough by draping it over branches of peeled green wood, fried dough prepared in the pan is more flavorful and more consistent in its texture. The outside cooks up just shy of crisp, while the inside retains its chewiness. The dough's short breadstick shape makes it ideal for dunking in either soup simmering in a pot over the coals, or in a small pot of jam or honey as a sweeter treat.

1 batch bread dough, such as Royal Dough (page 41) or Jaedo Havon (page 128)

½ cup (1 stick) salted butter

➤ MAKE UP YOUR BREAD DOUGH as instructed, and allow to rise for the first time until doubled in size. Punch down the dough and trim into pieces about 4 inches long and 1 inch wide. Twist these pieces of dough and set aside to rise for about 15 minutes, until slightly puffed again.

➤ WORKING IN BATCHES, melt a few tablespoons of the butter at a time in a large frying pan or skillet over medium heat. Fry several pieces of the twisted dough at a time, flipping occasionally, until golden brown and crisped on all sides, 6 to 8 minutes. Remove the fried breadsticks to a separate plate to cool somewhat.

Olive Loaf

MAKES: *1 large loaf*
PREP: *15 minutes*
RISING: *2 hours*
BAKING: *30 minutes*
PAIRS WELL WITH: *seasoned olive oil; Redwyne Roasted Grapes (page 68);*
Braavosi Pepperfish (page 61)

The culture and cuisine of Braavos were forged by hardship and determination. The city's founders—escaped slaves from many lands—created something from nothing when they fled into the swamps on the northern tip of Essos. Because of the varied backgrounds of its founders, Braavos boasts some of the most dynamic foods in all of Essos. As a youth, I visited the city with my father, and I still remember the marketplace filled with colorful breads and pastries piled in bright disarray. I begged my father to buy one, and he indulged me; one taste of this bread and I was lost. Years later, I commissioned a traveling novice to obtain the recipe I have included below.

The Braavosi use extra leavening to ensure that each loaf bakes up quite soft and airy, despite the dense lacing of olives and apricots. These impart a briny sweetness to the loaf that continues to entice, bite after bite. I've not been back to Braavos since that first visit, but I believe the recipe I have included is emblematic of many that one might find today in the markets and byways of the Titan's shadow. I like to think that the unusual combination of ingredients reflects the founders of Braavos itself: dissimilar in origin, but bound together to create something wonderful.

2 tablespoons honey
2 teaspoons instant dry yeast
1½ cups lukewarm water
2 teaspoons salt
¼ cup olive oil
½ cup chopped pitted Kalamata olives

½ cup diced dried apricots
2 teaspoons dried rosemary, savory, or
   thyme
3½ cups all-purpose flour
1 tablespoon cornmeal, for baking sheet

recipe continues

➤ **IN A LARGE BOWL,** combine the honey, yeast, and water.

➤ **ADD THE SALT,** olive oil, olives, apricots, and herbs, then stir in the flour 1 cup at a time, until the dough pulls away from the sides of the bowl and is not too sticky. Cover the bowl with plastic wrap or a damp towel, and allow the dough to rise for at least an hour, until it has about doubled in size.

➤ **PREHEAT THE OVEN** to 450°F and dust a large baking sheet with the cornmeal to keep the bread from sticking. Divide the dough into two equal pieces and form both into a long oval loaf shape. Place these on the baking sheet and allow to rise somewhere warm for another 30 minutes or so while the oven warms up. Just before baking, make several decorative slashes along the tops of the loaves with a sharp knife.

➤ **BAKE FOR ABOUT 30 MINUTES,** until the loaves are a nice golden brown and sound hollow when tapped. Allow to cool for another 20 minutes or so before slicing.

MAESTER'S NOTE *Green olives or a mixture of olives may also be used in this recipe, as suits your preference and what is available in the markets.*

Jaedo Havon

MAKES: *1 loaf of 8 servings*
PREP: *15 minutes*
RISING: *1½ hours*
BAKING: *25 minutes*
PAIRS WELL WITH: *soups and stews, specifically Dragonstone Jaerhilla (page 97);*
butter and jam

*J*aedo Havon means "summer loaf" in the old Valyrian tongue, and indeed the bread itself closely resembles the High Valyrian glyph for summer, as both invoke the shape of a blazing sun. Whether one takes its name from the other, or both hearken back to a much older word, we may never learn. Curiously, however, the distinctive sunburst pattern also has a practical explanation: the segments are formed by the practice of tying a piece of twine around each loaf, so that a single individual may more easily carry a great deal of bread at once. Although this style of bread is not seen in Westeros, it's common enough in Essos that bakeries often employ walking vendors to peddle the loaves, which they thread onto tall wooden racks that rest on their shoulders.

Slightly crisped on the outside and soft within, the loaf itself is divided into sections that can be easily pulled apart into individual servings. The medley of flours provides an earthier flavor than many of the loaves common to the Seven Kingdoms, while the seeds give the bread a little extra texture. Dipped in oil or spread with butter, this is a loaf that will not disappoint.

1 cup water
2 tablespoons honey
2 teaspoons instant dry yeast
2 cups spelt flour

2 cups wheat flour
2 teaspoons salt
2 tablespoons sesame seeds
1 tablespoon poppy seeds

➤ COMBINE THE WATER, honey, and yeast in a small bowl and allow to sit for a few minutes until foamy.

➤ IN A LARGE MIXING BOWL, combine the flours, salt, and seeds. Make a depression in the middle of these dry ingredients and pour the foamy yeast mixture into it. Stir, adding a little extra flour if needed, until you have a smooth dough that isn't too sticky. Turn the dough out onto a lightly floured work surface and knead for several minutes, until the dough bounces back when poked.

➤ LIGHTLY GREASE A LARGE BOWL with olive oil and place the dough in the bowl. Smooth any residual olive oil over the top of the dough, then cover the bowl with plastic wrap or a damp towel and set somewhere warm to rise for about an hour, until doubled in size.

➤ ONCE THE DOUGH HAS RISEN, preheat the oven to 400°F. Tip the dough out of the bowl onto a baking sheet lightly coated with olive oil, reshaping it into a round if needed. Tie a length of kitchen twine around the loaf, about halfway up its height and all the way around the outside, then knot the twine in a loop and trim off any excess. Let the dough rise for another 30 minutes or so, until somewhat puffy. Using a very sharp knife, score the top four times, to make eight equally sized wedges.

➤ BAKE FOR ABOUT 25 MINUTES, until the loaf is browned and sounds hollow when tapped. Let cool for at least 10 minutes before enjoying.

Cinnamon Swirled Loaf

MAKES: *1 loaf*
PREP: *40 minutes*
RISING: *1½ hours*
BAKING: *35 minutes*
PAIRS WELL WITH: *Seasoned Butter (page 34);*
Dothraki Dahanikh (page 48)

Early in my quest to discover extraordinary recipes, I traveled to King's Landing. Although I had ventured into the city many times to experience the rich cultural tapestry of street food, on this occasion I made the Red Keep and its library my main focus. One morning, when I sought to break my fast, I was surprised and delighted to receive several slices of this marvelous bread, slightly toasted and slathered with butter. It fortified me for the day, which began with an excited journey down to the kitchens.

At a glance, this loaf might be mistaken for an ordinary bread, but cut off a slice and you'll quickly see its true nature. A beautiful whorl of cinnamon spins outward from the center, while wine-stewed fruits are dotted throughout each slice. The taste is rich and rewarding, like the comfort of a hearth on a cold day.

1 cup red wine
½ cup sugar
1 tablespoon ground cinnamon
1 teaspoon ground nutmeg
Pinch of ground cloves

6 ounces (1½ cups) mixed dried fruit (such as currants, dates, raisins, etc.)
1 recipe Royal Dough (page 41)
2 tablespoons all-purpose flour
1 tablespoon unsalted butter, melted

➤ **COMBINE THE RED WINE,** ¼ cup of the sugar, ½ tablespoon of the cinnamon, ½ teaspoon of the nutmeg, and the cloves in a medium saucepan over medium heat. Add the dried fruit and cook for 20 to 30 minutes, until the fruit is soft and has absorbed most of the wine. Remove from the heat, strain the liquid in a separate container for future use (see Maester's Note), and allow the fruit to cool in the saucepan.

➤ **ONCE THE FRUIT HAS COOLED** to slightly warmer than room temperature, add it to the Royal Dough just before the addition of the flour asked for in that recipe. Allow the dough to rise as directed in the recipe.

➤ **ONCE THE DOUGH HAS RISEN,** roll it out into a rectangle about 8 inches wide and 16 inches long. Sprinkle the dough all over with the remaining sugar, cinnamon, nutmeg, and 2 tablespoons of flour. Working from one of the 8-inch sides, roll the dough up into a tube. Gently roll the tube a few times to seal the long end, then place it in a standard loaf pan. Brush the dough with the melted butter, and allow it to rise again at room temperature for about 30 minutes.

➤ **PREHEAT THE OVEN** to 350°F.

➤ **ONCE THE DOUGH HAS HAD ITS FINAL RISE,** bake it for about 35 minutes, until the top of the loaf is a rich brown color. Let the bread cool in the pan for at least 15 minutes before slicing.

MAESTER'S NOTE *The stewed fruit syrup is excellent stirred into hot water to make an infusion, or drizzled on top of griddlecakes, such as the Barley Griddlecakes (page 54) you'll find in this book.*

Ironborn Ship's Biscuits

MAKES: *About a dozen*
PREP: *10 minutes*
RISING: *10 minutes*
BAKING: *12 minutes*
PAIRS WELL WITH: *creamy cheese; smoked fish;*
Onion Broth with Carrot and Goat (page 94)

Ship's biscuits are found wherever men sail, but the ironborn have a particularly interesting variety. I was struck by their versatile approach, in which they use a medley of ingredients grown, gathered, and gleaned from raids. Thus, each batch is subtly different from one to the next. They generally include seaweed, rough grains, and plenty of salt. The biscuits can be softened by a soak in ale or broth, or even crumbled into boiling water to make a sort of gruel. These iron biscuits, as they are sometimes called, are also given to infants as they begin teething. Is it any wonder then, when some of their first tastes of food are salt and sea, that the ironborn take so readily to their ships?

I saw the making of these biscuits firsthand when I ventured down to the kitchens during a brief stay on Harlaw. They are generally produced by the salt wives and thralls of the ironborn, and in huge quantities. When baked through, they are wafer-thin and crisp. They are often strung onto leather thongs through the small hole in their middle and hung near the hearth to finish drying. Their seeds impart a much-needed flavor that is often lacking in such rations elsewhere, and I enjoyed them spread with a little soft goat's cheese and honey. They also make an exceptional pairing with a wide range of soups and stews.

1 cup rye flour
½ cup all-purpose flour
¼ cup rolled oats
¼ cup sesame seeds
1 teaspoon fennel seeds

1 teaspoon caraway seeds
¼ cup finely chopped dried wakame seaweed
1 teaspoon salt
1 tablespoon cider vinegar
¾ cup water

➤ PREHEAT THE OVEN to 400°F and set out a baking sheet.

➤ COMBINE THE DRY INGREDIENTS in a medium mixing bowl, toss in the seaweed followed by the cider vinegar, and then add just a little of the water at a time, mixing well after each addition until you have a nice dough that isn't too sticky to handle. Transfer the dough to a lightly floured surface and knead until it is smooth and firm. Set the dough aside on the counter to rest for about 10 minutes.

➤ USING LIGHTLY FLOURED HANDS, divide the dough into 12 equal pieces and roll each piece into a ball. On a lightly floured surface, roll each ball into a thin disc about 6 inches across, adding more flour as needed to prevent the dough from sticking. Poke a little hole in the middle of each disc if you plan to string your biscuits up after they bake, then move the discs to the baking sheet. Bake for about 12 minutes, until the biscuits are just turning golden at the edges.

➤ TO REALLY CRISP UP THE BISCUITS, turn off the oven, then leave the pan in the oven with the door cracked until the biscuits are completely cooled, about an hour. Or you can do as the ironborn do and string them up somewhere to dry.

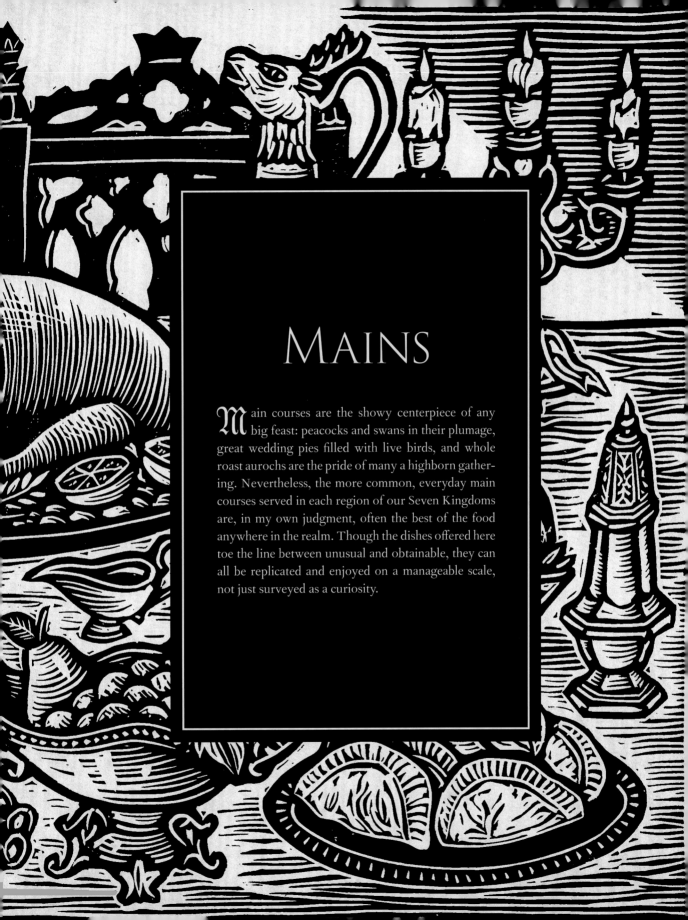

Mains

Main courses are the showy centerpiece of any big feast: peacocks and swans in their plumage, great wedding pies filled with live birds, and whole roast aurochs are the pride of many a highborn gathering. Nevertheless, the more common, everyday main courses served in each region of our Seven Kingdoms are, in my own judgment, often the best of the food anywhere in the realm. Though the dishes offered here toe the line between unusual and obtainable, they can all be replicated and enjoyed on a manageable scale, not just surveyed as a curiosity.

Highgarden Dumplings

MAKES: *4 servings*
PREP: *20 minutes*
COOKING: *40 minutes*
PAIRS WELL WITH: *white wine; Lace Wafer Cookies (page 188)*

Nowhere in the Seven Kingdoms can boast such rich harvests or such flavorful produce as the Reach. Perhaps there is some truth to the legends of Garth Greenhand and his agrarian powers, but more likely the fertility of the lands around Highgarden can be attributed to the more mundane properties of its soil and geography. Regardless, so great is the bounty of the Reach that without its exports, much of Westeros would go hungry. One happy consequence of these plentiful harvests is that cooks and farmwives throughout the region are endlessly dreaming up new ways to employ their bounty.

One of my favorite dishes, rarely seen anywhere but the south, is a small dumpling made with either squash or beetroot. The recipe is straightforward: the vegetables are roasted until soft, then blended with flour and an egg to make a dough that can be cut small and boiled. The resulting bite-size dumplings are soft and a little chewy. Sauced with butter, herbs, and cheese, it's a memorable combination that plates beautifully for honored guests.

1 pound (about 2 cups) butternut squash,
   peeled and cubed
2 tablespoons olive oil
1 egg
¼ cup grated Parmesan cheese
½ teaspoon ground nutmeg
1½ to 2 cups all-purpose flour

BROWN BUTTER SAUCE
½ cup (1 stick) unsalted butter
Small handful of fresh sage leaves, roughly
   chopped
½ cup heavy cream
¼ cup toasted walnuts, roughly chopped
½ cup cooked peas
Salt and ground black pepper
Grated Parmesan cheese, for serving

recipe continues

➤ **PREHEAT THE OVEN** to 400°F. Toss the squash with the olive oil and spread out on a baking sheet. Roast in the oven for about 25 minutes, flipping the squash halfway through, until very tender.

➤ **WHILE THE SQUASH IS COOKING,** make the sauce: Melt the butter over medium-low heat in a large frying pan, stirring occasionally. After several minutes, it should become foamy and start to turn a nutty brown color. Reduce the heat to low, add in the sage, and then stir in the heavy cream. Let cook for several minutes, until somewhat thickened. Remove from the heat and stir in the walnuts and peas. Season to taste with salt and pepper.

➤ **ONCE THE SQUASH IS COOKED,** add it to a medium mixing bowl and allow it to cool for several minutes. Add the egg and puree with an immersion blender until smooth (the squash may also be mashed by hand, but the texture might be more rustic). Add in the Parmesan and nutmeg. Gradually add in 1½ cups of the flour, then, if needed, continue to add flour until you have formed a dough that is not sticky and can be kneaded. Turn the dough out onto a lightly floured surface and knead until smooth.

➤ **BRING A LARGE POT** of salted water to a boil. Divide the dough into quarters and, still working on the lightly floured surface, roll each quarter out into a rope that is no more than ½ inch thick, then cut each rope into sections about 1 inch long. Once all the dough has been cut, add the dumplings to the boiling water in batches of four. Allow the dumplings to cook for several minutes, until they are all floating at the top of the water, then scoop them out with a slotted spoon and drain them.

➤ **ADD THE COOKED DUMPLINGS** to the sauce and stir to coat. Serve warm and top with extra Parmesan cheese, if desired.

Dothraki Blood Pies

MAKES: *About a dozen*
PREP: *20 minutes*
COOKING: *20 minutes*
PAIRS WELL WITH: *sweet milky tea; kefir or Dothraki Pepper Beer Syrup (page 218); grilled vegetables*

When a Dothraki khalasar ends a long day's ride, there is a flurry of activity as they make camp. Horses are tended to, tents erected, and cookfires lit. Before long, the smell of cooking meat wends its way through the air, mingling with the scents of horse and human sweat—the essence of Dothraki on the move. As their nomadic lifestyle precludes the use of ovens, all the hot meals the Dothraki consume are cooked quickly on spits, or in pots over cookfires fed with dried grasses and dung. While this approach might seem primitive to some, it results in food that is practical yet still highly flavorful, and each dish I've had the pleasure of tasting surprised and delighted my senses.

Such was the case with these blood pies. The simple dough fries up to a crisp golden brown on the outside while remaining somewhat chewy throughout. It envelops a savory filling of ground lamb and blood sausage laced with spices, with sharp bursts of garlic and onion providing a heat that builds the longer one eats.

FILLING
1 tablespoon olive oil
2 garlic cloves, minced
1 small yellow onion, minced
8 ounces ground lamb
8 ounces raw blood sausage, roughly chopped
1 teaspoon Aleppo pepper, or to taste
1 teaspoon ground cumin, or to taste
2 tablespoons all-purpose flour

DOUGH
2¼ cups all-purpose flour
½ teaspoon salt
¾ cup warm water

recipe continues

➤ To MAKE THE FILLING, combine all the ingredients in a large bowl and set aside.

➤ To MAKE THE DOUGH, mix the flour and salt in a medium mixing bowl. Add just enough of the water to mix up a smooth dough that can be kneaded a few times without getting sticky, then divide the dough into twelve equal pieces.

➤ ROLL OUT THE DOUGH one piece at a time into thin circles about 6 inches across. Spread 3 to 4 tablespoons of the filling over the dough, leaving ½ inch bare around the edges. Fold each circle in half and crimp the edges together with your fingers or the tines of a fork.

➤ HEAT 2 INCHES OF VEGETABLE OIL in a large frying pan over medium-high heat until shimmering and line a large plate with paper towels. Lower a few hand pies at a time into the hot oil and cook for about 5 minutes, flipping occasionally, until all sides of the pies are a rich golden brown and the meat is cooked through. Remove to the plate lined with paper towels to drain, and serve while still warm.

MAESTER'S NOTE *A few dollops of tangy goat cheese mixed into the filling can add extra depth and flavor. The blood sausage is what makes this dish truly special, but if it is out of season or otherwise unavailable, your next favorite sausage may be substituted. The flavor, however, will not be comparable to the original.*

Pease Pie
Laced with Bacon

MAKES: *1 pie of about 8 servings*
PREP: *15 minutes*
BAKING: *30 minutes*
PAIRS WELL WITH: *Boiled Beans with Bacon (page 77);*
Beef and Barley Soup (page 108); ale or white wine

Pies are a common offering throughout much of Westeros, but they're especially popular in the cooler northern climates where they offer a delicious way to serve up vegetables and meat that have been preserved for the long winters. Pease, likewise, seem among the most common staples of the Westerosi pantry, though they're consumed mostly by the smallfolk. High in protein, they can be dried and stored almost indefinitely, making them a popular choice for hedge knights, merchants, and those who spend much time on the road. In some of the southern regions of the continent, pease are considered a lowly crop, little better than fodder for livestock. But even the proudest lord may learn to love the humble pea when his stores run dry near the end of a long winter. The North seems to have embraced these little legumes wholeheartedly, however, from hovel to high hall, where they are frequently seen gracing the tables of feasts alongside more exotic offerings.

In this recipe, a soft pastry crust encircles a well of vibrant fresh peas made creamy by the addition of tangy goat cheese. Small pieces of bacon scattered sporadically throughout the dish add a savory element to nearly every bite. This is one of the simpler recipes for pease pie, but I have encountered others in many an inn and hall with more varied seasonings: wild boar substituted for the bacon, sharper cheeses that form a crust over the top, and so forth. In each case, the finished dish reflects what is available to each cook, and the preferences of those to whom it is served.

1 batch Brown Butter Pastry Crust dough
   (page 22)
16 ounces fresh (or frozen and thawed) peas
8 ounces goat cheese

1 egg
1 tablespoon lemon juice or cider vinegar
Salt and ground black pepper
4 bacon strips, cooked crisp and crumbled

➻ **PREHEAT THE OVEN** to 375°F. Make and roll out the pastry dough. Lay it gently over a 9-inch pie or tart pan, pressing it into the bottom and edges of the pan. Trim off any excess dough and set it aside to make crust decorations, if you wish.

➻ **SET A MEDIUM SAUCEPAN** filled halfway with water over medium-high heat. Once it's simmering, add the peas and cook for several minutes, until the peas are soft and a vibrant green color. Drain the peas and pour about two-thirds of them into a large mixing bowl. Add the goat cheese, egg, and lemon juice to the bowl, then puree with an immersion blender until smooth and season with the salt and pepper. Stir in the remaining peas and crumbled bacon. Pour the filling into the pastry shell, and top with the optional pastry decorations. Bake for 25 to 30 minutes, until the edges of the pastry are turning a golden brown and the center of the pie is set. Serve warm or cool.

White Harbor Meat Pie

MAKES: *1 pie of about 8 servings*
PREP: *15 minutes*
COOKING: *1 hour*
PAIRS WELL WITH: *strong northern ale;*
Boiled Beans with Bacon (page 77)

Meat pies have been popular in the North as far back as we have records, and it is said that the North remembers the ways of the First Men. Without a doubt, there are many inns and lordly homes that boast that their savory pies are the best in the region—or perhaps in all of Westeros. Although I have not had the good fortune to examine all the claims personally, I suspect that were an exhaustive investigation completed, the honor would probably fall upon the Manderlys of White Harbor, who set as rich a table as any southern lord. When I visited the New Castle, I was welcomed almost as family; Lord Manderly, perhaps sensing in me a kindred spirit when it came to the delights of the table, ensured that every meal we enjoyed together was a small feast. When I mentioned this pie was my particular favorite, he was kind enough to put his cooks at my disposal with instructions to share whatever information I might require.

With its sturdy pastry casing stuffed to the brim with flavorful filling, this savory pie is the best example of the meat pie breed. Myriad vegetables swim through a thick, dark gravy, offering up the earthy flavors of carrot, turnip, and parsnip interspersed with the occasional sweet pop of a pearl onion. Chunks of savory pork or other meats provide additional substance. While this pie makes for excellent cold weather fare, it would make a fine addition to an evening spread in any season.

8 ounces pork belly, diced large (thick-cut
   bacon could also work)
2 pounds pork tenderloin, cut into
   1-inch cubes
6 tablespoons salted/unsalted butter
½ cup peeled and chopped carrots
½ cup pearl onions
1 medium turnip, peeled and chopped
½ cup chopped parsnips
1 cup button mushrooms

1½ cups beef broth
Hearty pinch of salt
3 tablespoons all-purpose flour
1½ cups dark beer
2 batches Brown Butter Pastry Crust dough
   (page 22)
Hearty pinch of ground black pepper
Hearty pinch of savory dried herbs, such as
   thyme, rosemary, savory, etc.
1 egg

➤ **In a large skillet** or frying pan, toss the pork belly over medium heat until it's cooked through, 6 to 8 minutes. Set the pork belly aside in a large bowl, reserving any fat in the pan. Add the cubed pork to the pan and gently sear until each piece is browned. Transfer the meat to the same bowl as the pork belly and set aside.

➤ **In the same pan** that was used for the pork, melt 3 tablespoons of the butter over medium heat and add the vegetables. Add a splash of the broth and the salt, then cover and let simmer until the vegetables are soft, 10 to 15 minutes. Pour everything into the bowl with the meat.

➤ **In the same pan,** melt the remaining 3 tablespoons of butter over medium heat and add the flour, stirring until the mixture is a nice golden color. While stirring, gradually pour in the remaining broth and the beer, alternating between the two until the mixture reaches a nice, thick consistency. Pour the vegetables and the meat back into the pan and let cook for another minute or two, while stirring, until the whole mixture is covered with the thick gravy. Remove from the heat and allow to cool.

➤ **Divide the pastry dough in two,** then roll it about ¼ inch thick. Drape half the dough over a standard 9-inch pie dish and add the cooled filling. Add a pinch each of black pepper and savory dried herbs. Top with the other half of the rolled dough, trim and crimp the edges, and brush with an egg beaten with a little water. Poke a few small holes in the top of the pie as vents, and cook for about an hour, until the crust is golden.

Roast Goose
Sauced with Mulberries

MAKES: *About 6 servings*
PREP: *15 minutes*
COOKING: *2 hours*
SAUCE: *15 minutes*
PAIRS WELL WITH: *Valyrian Gingerbread (page 195); Hippocras (page 200)*

Geese are an essential resource throughout Westeros. Their feathers are used for arrow fletching, quills, and the stuffing of pillows, and many smallfolk make brooms from their wings. But most important for my purposes, their meat is rich and delicious in any season. In fact, the popularity of goose at lordly tables means that those who raise the birds (which are considerably more labor-intensive than chickens) rarely get to eat them; the flesh is simply too valuable not to sell.

For me, this particular dish conjures memories of early autumn in the crownlands, when the sun licks the first taste of frost from the late summer apples, and the smell of woodsmoke lingers in the lowlands. The dark meat of the goose is rich and sumptuous against the mulberry sauce, which adds a sour-sweet snap of vinegar and fruit. The ground almonds and bread crumbs introduce a rustic texture, making the dish well-suited to an afternoon spread enjoyed out of doors. But whether under the broad sky or the timbered ceiling of a lordly hall, this dish is guaranteed to please even the most discerning guest.

1 whole goose (about 10 pounds)
Coarse salt
4 apples, cored and diced
About 3 cups cubed stale bread
1 cup dried currants
¼ cup (½ stick) salted/unsalted butter, melted

1 garlic clove, minced
Generous pinch of thyme
Generous pinch of marjoram
Salt and ground black pepper
Mulberry Sauce (recipe follows)

➤ PREHEAT THE OVEN to 350°F and wash the goose inside and out. Pat the bird dry with towels, and arrange it on a roasting tray. Cut off the excess neck fat, then prick the skin all over with a sharp knife or skewer, which will help drain the fat. Sprinkle liberally with the coarse salt on all sides.

➤ IN A LARGE MIXING BOWL, combine all the remaining ingredients to make the stuffing, seasoning to taste with the salt and pepper. Stuff the bird, tucking the wings in to keep them from burning.

➤ ROAST FOR 2 HOURS, then check the goose: if the juices run clear from the thigh, then it should be done. As the legs often need a little more time than the body, however, it's all right to take the goose out after 1½ hours or so, carve the breast meat off, then continue to cook the legs until they are done. Periodically remove the fat from the roasting tray with a baster, straining and reserving it for future use. When the goose is done, allow it to rest for at least 10 minutes before carving. Serve with the sauce below.

Mulberry Sauce

MAKES: *About 2 cups*

2 cups fresh mulberries
Red wine vinegar
½ cup ground almonds

¼ cup bread crumbs
Pinch each of ground ginger, pepper, and
   nutmeg

➤ PLACE THE MULBERRIES in a medium saucepan and roughly mash them. Add a splash of vinegar, and let simmer over medium-low heat until the berries have broken down, 15 to 20 minutes. Strain the juices into a clean bowl, pressing on the pulp to extract as much juice as possible, then discard the fruit.

➤ RETURN THE JUICE to the saucepan and add the almonds, bread crumbs, and spices. Gradually add a little more of the vinegar until you have a suitably runny consistency for a sauce. Simmer for a few minutes, then remove from the heat and set aside. This sauce is best served warm.

MAESTER'S NOTE *If mulberries are not to be found where you live, other fruit such as blackberries or blueberries may be substituted. The rendered goose fat can be used to roast vegetables to excellent effect.*

Crown Roast
of Boar's Ribs

MAKES: *1 roast of about 4 servings*
PREP: *30 minutes*
COOKING: *2 hours*
PAIRS WELL WITH: *Riverlands Creamed Leeks (page 87);*
Hippocras (page 200)

here is a saying in Westeros: Heavy is the head that wears the crown. But heavy also is the feast table that bears this impressive centerpiece. Crown Roast was a specialty of the head cook in the Red Keep in the early days of King Robert's reign. He was called Oswyn, and he was good enough to speak with me at great length about the demands and opportunities inherent in feeding a royal household. I heard his account of expansive versions of this dish made with aurochs ribs—roasts so huge a grown man could stand in them with room to spare. The recipe below is a much more reasonable size, suitable for an intimate dinner or for making an impression on a small party of guests.

As a son of the stormlands, King Robert generally preferred venison or boar to aurochs. This hearty roast is ideal cold weather fare, with a dense oaten stuffing laced with bacon and fruit. The meat slow cooks until it just about falls from the bones in a delicious heap. The spice blend dances over the roast, pairing beautifully with both the crisped bacon and the rib meat. Each bite of the soft stuffing that fills the hollow crown hides small bites of apple and onion kissed by herbs. It is a splendid meal that leaves one sated and happy.

1 rack (about 4 pounds) boar or pork ribs
1½ tablespoons Freehold Spice Blend
   (page 24), or spice rub of your choice
About 5 uncooked bacon strips

STUFFING

2 cups rolled oats, soaked for 30 minutes
   and drained
¼ cup dried currants
About 3 uncooked bacon strips
3 tablespoons unsalted butter
1 yellow onion, diced small
½ apple, cored and diced
2 garlic cloves, minced
1 tablespoon chopped fresh parsley
½ teaspoon dried thyme
½ cup chicken or beef stock
2 slices stale bread, torn into small pieces

recipe continues

➤ PREHEAT THE OVEN to 375°F.

➤ USING A SHARP KNIFE, carefully trim away the meat from the top 1 to 2 inches of the ribs and set the scraps aside to use later. Curve the rack of ribs around itself and set upright with the bulk of the meat at the bottom. Secure the ends together either with toothpicks or by tying some kitchen twine around the whole roast. Dust the inside and outside of the meat with the spice blend. Wrap several strips of bacon around the circumference of the roast, then place it on a large, rimmed baking sheet. Set aside while you prepare the stuffing.

➤ TO MAKE THE STUFFING, pour the oats and currants into a medium saucepan and cover with several inches of water. Set over medium heat and bring to a simmer. Cook for about 15 minutes, until the oats have softened. Drain and transfer the oat mixture to a large mixing bowl.

➤ WHILE THE OATS COOK, mince the scraps of meat trimmed from the roast. Fry the bacon and the minced meat together in a medium frying pan over medium heat until the bacon is crispy. Drain the meat, reserving a bit of the fat in the pan for later. Allow the meats to cool before crumbling the bacon and adding both meats to the oats.

➤ IN THE SAME PAN you used to cook the bacon, melt the butter with the remaining bacon fat over medium heat. Add the onion, apple, and garlic and cook for several minutes, until the onion is soft and fragrant. Turn down the heat and add the herbs, followed by the stock. Stir for a minute, then remove from the heat and add to the oat mixture along with the bread. Mix everything together thoroughly.

➤ PRESS THE STUFFING into the center of the crown roast atop the baking sheet, making a little dome in the middle of the stuffing. Cover with aluminum foil and move the roast to the oven. Cook for around 2 hours, until the bacon is crisp and the meat ready to fall from the bones. About 20 minutes before the end of the cooking time, remove the foil to allow the stuffing to brown a little.

➤ TO SERVE, snip away the twine, cut the roast vertically into chops, and plate the chops with some of the stuffing.

CHELSEA'S NOTE *The stuffing used here can also be prepared on its own as a side. Simply bake in a large casserole dish for around 30 minutes at 350°F until cooked through and browning on top, stirring occasionally to avoid any overly crispy bits.*

Boiled Beef
with Horseradish Sauce

MAKES: *4 to 6 large servings*
PREP: *5 minutes*
COOKING: *About 3 hours*
PAIRS WELL WITH: *sharp cheddar cheese; crusty bread;*
red wine or beer; Stewed Plums (page 175)

Even for the highborn, raising animals for meat is an expensive endeavor, so prudent stewards see to it that little is wasted. Nevertheless, some cuts of meat may be too tough even for roasting, while others might be overly fatty or harvested from animals too old for good flavor. Clever cooks know their way around the butcher's block—and the tricks for preparing every part of a beast, from nose to tail, to best advantage. Techniques such as boiling are especially important for making the most of what each animal has to offer, without having to endure unpleasant meals for the sake of effective household management.

Too brothy to be a stew, this dish falls more in the realm of main courses—albeit a lighter one. The meat slow cooks for several hours until quite tender, all while swimming in a broth of spices and herbs that lend it extra depth. The addition of horseradish sauce upon serving lends a welcome extra snap. Some cooks put root vegetables into the broth near the end of the cooking process, but I prefer the meaty broth unadulterated.

2 pounds beef stew meat
½ cup red wine vinegar
2 teaspoons salt
3 to 5 whole garlic cloves
2 tablespoons molasses or honey
½ teaspoon dried savory
½ teaspoon Stag's Spice (page 25)

HORSERADISH SAUCE
1½ tablespoons salted/unsalted butter
1½ tablespoons all-purpose flour
3 tablespoons grated horseradish
¼ cup heavy cream
Salt and ground black pepper

➤ **Place the meat** in a medium pot along with the vinegar, salt, garlic, molasses, and seasonings. Add enough water to cover the meat by 2 inches and place over medium heat. Once the water has reached a rolling boil, reduce the heat to medium-low and cover. Cook for 2½ hours or until the meat is tender, checking occasionally to make sure the meat is still submerged, and adding more water as needed if it is not. Transfer the meat to a bowl and keep warm, reserving the broth for the sauce and any leftover meat (see Maester's Note).

➤ **To make the sauce,** melt the butter in a medium saucepan over medium heat, then add the flour and stir to combine. Cook for a minute or so, until the mixture turns a nice golden color. While stirring, add in 1 cup of reserved broth. Stir to combine and continue cooking as the mixture thickens. Add the horseradish, simmer for a few minutes, then remove the pan from the heat and add the cream.

➤ **Season to taste** with the salt and pepper, then add to the cooked meat and serve (see Maester's Note).

MAESTER'S NOTE *If any meat remains after serving, I recommend returning it to the broth and continuing to cook it over a low fire until the broth has reduced and the meat can be easily shredded. This may be served over toasted bread for a hearty breakfast the following day.*

Stargazy Pie

MAKES: *1 pie of about 8 servings*
PREP: *20 minutes*
BAKING: *40 minutes*
PAIRS WELL WITH: *Jaedo Havon (page 128); Valyrian Gingerbread (page 195)*

The notes attached to this particular recipe from the King's Landing archives indicate that this fish pie was first served at a banquet celebrating the successful return of the Sea Snake, Corlys Velaryon, from one of his many profitable voyages to Essos. Subsequently, many lesser nobles along Westeros's eastern coast adopted the recipe in their own halls, and it eventually made its way to King's Landing. It is perhaps one of the more striking dishes to grace a table, largely due to the creative use of the fish heads, which point upward from the crust as if marveling at the starry sky above, giving the dish its unique name. Pies such as this are sometimes made as large as wagon wheels, bursting with entire schools of fish.

The pie itself is packed with chunks of whitefish swimming in a thick creamy sauce, made smoky by the addition of bacon. Chopped leeks, onions, and boiled eggs join the fish to give the sauce considerably more body and flavor. The fish heads roast up to a satisfying crispness and are more for show than for eating, although the bones of smaller fish make a satisfying crunch for more adventurous eaters.

6 (about 2 pounds) whitefish (such as
    whiting, mackerel, smelt, or another fish
    of a similar size), butterflied with heads on
4 uncooked bacon strips, diced
1 tablespoon salted/unsalted butter
1 leek, white part only, diced
1 medium yellow onion, diced

About ¼ cup flour
1 cup chicken broth
½ cup heavy cream
3 hard-boiled eggs, roughly chopped
1 heaping tablespoon minced parsley
About 1 pound puff pastry dough

recipe continues

➤ **PREHEAT THE OVEN** to 400°F. Chop the heads from the fish just below the gills and set the heads aside. Roughly chop the rest of the fish and set aside. Lightly butter a standard 9-inch pie dish and, likewise, set to the side.

➤ **ADD THE BACON** to a large frying pan over medium heat. Cook until the bacon is crisp and dark. Move the bacon to a separate plate and drain all but about 1 tablespoon of the bacon grease from the pan. Add the butter to the pan, followed by the leek and onion. Cook for several minutes, until the vegetables have softened and are fragrant. Sprinkle with the flour and stir until the flour has been absorbed. Gradually pour in the broth, followed by the heavy cream, continuing to cook until you have a nice thick sauce. Stir in the chopped fish as well as the boiled eggs and parsley.

➤ **POUR THIS FILLING** into the prepared pie dish, spreading it out evenly. Carefully lower the dough on top of the dish and trim off any excess crust. Cut six small slits into the dough and insert the reserved fish heads into the slits, so the heads appear to be gazing up at the stars. Bake for about 40 minutes, until the pastry is a rich golden color. Allow to cool for about 15 minutes before slicing. The pie will be runny, more like a stew with a pastry top, so a large serving spoon and bowls are advisable.

Tenderloin Skewers

MAKES: *4 to 6 servings*
PREP: *15 minutes*
COOKING: *20 minutes*
PAIRS WELL WITH: *rice or couscous; Rhoynish Pudding (page 194);*
Mead (page 203)

J know of few dishes fit for a high lord's table that can be as easily prepared over a campfire in the kingswood as they can be in a fully appointed castle kitchen, but this is one. Skewered meats and vegetables have long been popular choices among hedge knights, whose means of cooking are oft limited to a few choice implements. As such, I found it no surprise to discover that this recipe was prevalent during the reign of King Aegon V and was marked "for the king's table" in the royal archives. One can easily imagine Aegon's fondness for the dish stemming from his days traveling as a hedge knight's squire.

The means of cooking this dish are quite clever. By interspersing the beef with fattier cuts of bacon, the meat stays completely moist as it cooks and takes on the bacon's rich saltiness, while interspersed leaves of sage add an herbal note. The beef can be eaten directly from the skewers or removed to a serving platter.

1 to 2 (about 5 pounds) beef tenderloins
½ cup grape juice
¼ cup red wine vinegar
1 teaspoon fennel pollen or ground
   fennel seed

Hefty pinch of salt
¼ teaspoon ground black pepper
1 pound uncooked bacon or salt pork, cut
   into squares
Generous handful of fresh sage leaves

➤ CUT THE TENDERLOIN into large chunks. Place the meat in a deep ovenproof dish, then pour the grape juice, vinegar, fennel pollen, salt, and pepper on top. Press the meat down and let it marinate, covered in the fridge, for several hours.

➤ HEAT THE BROILER TO LOW. When ready to cook, slide the meat onto long skewers interspersed by the bacon and sage leaves, and reserve the marinade. Broil the skewers on low for about 15 minutes, until the meat is just done, flipping the skewers about halfway through; the meat should be brown on the outside with a hint of pink within. Transfer the skewers to a large plate and cover to keep warm, then pour the drippings from the ovenproof dish into a medium frying pan.

➤ ADD THE REMAINING MARINADE to the frying pan and cook over medium heat until the mixture thickens somewhat, a few minutes. Drizzle the sauce over the skewers and serve them warm.

CHELSEA'S NOTE *Tenderloin works well for this recipe, but steak tips are another great option.*

Pentoshi Honeyed Duck

MAKES: *1 duck, about 4 medium servings*
PREP: *15 minutes*
COOKING: *2½ hours*
PAIRS WELL WITH: *mead or honeyed wine; risotto;*
roasted vegetables; Volantene Ale (page 213)

Among the nobility of Pentos, hospitality is considered something of a competitive sport, and it reflects their deeper political games. Each magister is eager to outdo the next, since a bountiful table is suggestive of economic strength. I have seen exotic birds presented in their plumage, whole menageries made of gilded sweets, and elaborate edible centerpieces that could be made to move with the turn of a crank. So the below dish is but a humble offering as far as Pentoshi recipes go, but I still found it well worth the eating.

The duck roasts to a perfect crispness as the fat melts away, leaving a layer of flaky skin surrounding the incredibly moist and tender flesh within. The meat is seasoned from the inside out by the oranges, imparting a flavor that is echoed in the sultry sauce. Exotic spices further deepen the experience, their expense providing yet another show of wealth with each bite.

One 4-pound whole duck, rinsed
1 teaspoon ground cardamom
1 teaspoon ground ginger
Pinch of white pepper
¼ teaspoon ground cumin
1 teaspoon salt
1 orange, quartered

SAUCE
1 cup honey
½ cup (1 stick) unsalted butter
1 teaspoon lemon juice
½ cup orange juice
Pinch of Aleppo pepper

➤ **PREHEAT THE OVEN** to 350°F and set out a roasting pan.

➤ **TO PREPARE THE DUCK,** prick the skin all over with a sharp knife; this will allow some of the fat to run out and keep the duck from getting too greasy. Reserve the rendered duck fat after cooking for use in other recipes.

➤ **IN A SMALL BOWL,** mix the spices and salt. Sprinkle this mixture over the skin of the duck and stuff the inside of the duck with the orange quarters. Place the duck on the roasting pan breast-side up and move to the oven.

➤ **COOK THE DUCK** for 30 minutes, then turn the duck breast-side down and reduce the heat to 300°F. Cook for another 2 hours, or until the duck is dark golden in color. If desired, turn the duck breast-side up again near the end of the 2 hours to brown the other side.

➤ **MAKE THE SAUCE** while the duck cooks: simmer the honey, butter, lemon juice, and orange juice in a small saucepan until the honey and butter have melted, and all the ingredients have combined with one another. Pour a splash of this over the duck before returning the bird to the oven. Serve the duck with the remaining sauce.

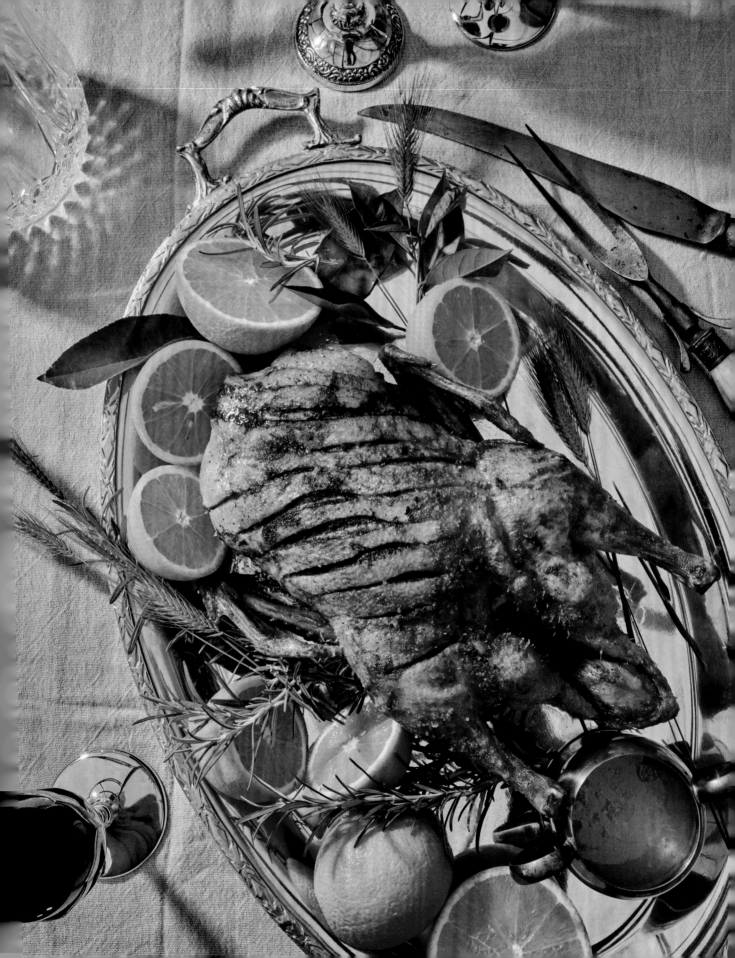

Mutton Chops
Sauced with Honey and Spice

MAKES: *2 servings*
MARINATE: *2 hours (or longer)*
COOKING: *About 20 minutes*
PAIRS WELL WITH: *dark bread; Poppyseed Pastries (page 184);*
Myrish Firewine (page 210)

Although the Reach may boast some incredibly flavorful lamb dishes, the North has mastered the art of cooking mutton into something truly wonderful. While southern lamb is lightly flavored with delicate seasonings, the northern recipes highlight the flavors inherent in the mutton itself, enhancing them with strong sauces and spices. I enjoyed my first taste of mutton chops in honey during a visit to Winterfell, just before the first snows, and was immediately struck by the complexity of the dish.

These mutton chops are a popular dish in the North come autumn, when the herds are being culled for the coming winter. But as mutton is often tougher than lamb, a marinade is vital to soften the meat. A marinade of dark beer, mixed with a northern honey that carries the delicate taste of summer wildflower meadows, is rendered into a thick, sweet sauce enhanced with just a hint of spice. The meat cooks quickly to tenderness, and its robust flavor is complemented beautifully by the sauce. Although a touch heavy for summer, it's an ideal dish for cold weather.

2 tablespoons unsalted butter
2 shallots, sliced thin
1 tablespoon brown sugar
1 cup dark beer, such as milk stout
3 tablespoons honey

⅛ teaspoon ground cloves
⅛ teaspoon ground cinnamon
1 bay leaf
6 mutton chops
Dash of cider vinegar

➤ **MELT 1 TABLESPOON** of the butter in a medium frying pan over medium heat. Add the shallots and cook for several minutes, until soft and fragrant. Stir in the brown sugar and cook for a few more minutes, until the shallots are quite soft and browned. Remove from the heat and combine with the beer, honey, cloves, cinnamon, and bay leaf in a medium bowl to create a marinade. Allow to cool for a few minutes.

➤ **PLACE THE MEAT** in a small glass container, then pour on the marinade. Place the container in the fridge and let it sit uncovered for at least 2 hours (see Maester's Note).

➤ **WHEN READY TO COOK,** melt the remaining 1 tablespoon of butter in a medium frying pan over medium-high heat. Transfer the mutton to the pan and sear for about a minute on each side, then pour in the marinade and reduce the heat slightly. Cook the mutton in the marinade for another 4 minutes or so on each side, then remove the mutton and keep warm. Continue to cook the sauce until it has noticeably thickened, 5 to 10 minutes. Drizzle over the mutton to serve.

MAESTER'S NOTE *If pressed for time, the marinating step may be skipped without much ill effect.*

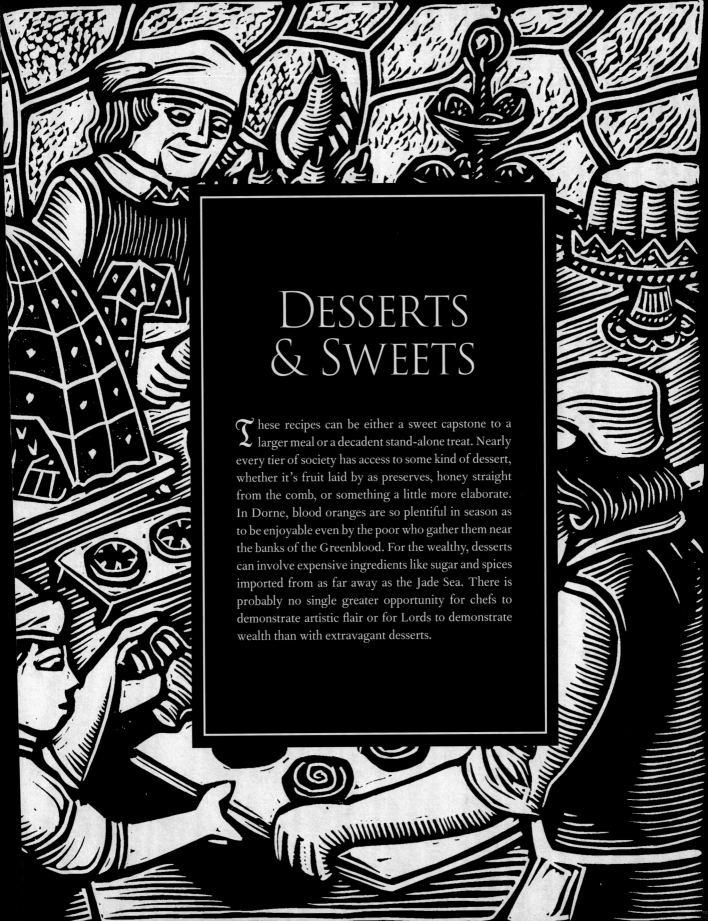

Desserts & Sweets

These recipes can be either a sweet capstone to a larger meal or a decadent stand-alone treat. Nearly every tier of society has access to some kind of dessert, whether it's fruit laid by as preserves, honey straight from the comb, or something a little more elaborate. In Dorne, blood oranges are so plentiful in season as to be enjoyable even by the poor who gather them near the banks of the Greenblood. For the wealthy, desserts can involve expensive ingredients like sugar and spices imported from as far away as the Jade Sea. There is probably no single greater opportunity for chefs to demonstrate artistic flair or for Lords to demonstrate wealth than with extravagant desserts.

Stewed Plums

MAKES: *4 servings*
PREP: *5 minutes*
COOKING: *15 minutes*
PAIRS WELL WITH: *roasted game meat; almond biscuits;*
port wine or Hippocras (page 200); yogurt and granola

Plums are harvested throughout much of Westeros, but especially in the southern regions, where they flourish during the summer growing season. Fireplums are a specialty that grow only in the Reach, but they're famed far and wide for their deep purple hue and rich flavor that is perfectly complemented by warming spices. Most varieties can be dried and preserved for the long winters ahead, but fresh fireplums are used in this dish to make use of the summer bounty in a celebration of the season.

This recipe can be adapted somewhat to achieve two different purees: yellow plums and white wine yield a golden-colored mousse, while purple plums and a red wine form a rich, red-hued sauce. The plums can also be sliced, stewed, and served in pieces, if you prefer more texture with every bite.

About 1 pound purple or yellow plums
1⅓ cups wine (red wine for purple plums,
    white wine for yellow plums)
¼ cup honey, or more to taste
1 tablespoon rice flour

Pinch of salt
Pinch of Stag's Spice (page 25)
    or five-spice powder
Candied citrus peel and/or aniseed, to
    garnish (optional)

➤ WASH AND PIT THE PLUMS, cutting them into small pieces. Bring the wine to a boil in a medium saucepan over medium-high heat. Reduce the heat to a simmer and add the plums. Cook for about 5 minutes, until the plums are very soft. Pour about ¼ cup of the wine from the pan and set aside, then puree the plums and the remaining wine with an immersion blender until completely smooth. Stir in the honey.

➤ IN A SMALL BOWL, combine the rice flour with the reserved ¼ cup of wine, then add to the plum puree. Add the salt and Stag's Spice and return to low heat to cook for about 10 minutes, until the whole mixture has thickened. If desired, garnish with candied citrus peel and/or aniseed. Cool only slightly before serving—these plums are best enjoyed still warm.

MAESTER'S NOTE: *If you prefer to keep the fruit in pieces, feel free to skip the pureeing step.*

Apple Crisps

MAKES: *About 4 servings*
PREP: *35 minutes*
FRYING: *30 minutes*
PAIRS WELL WITH: *sparkling hard cider;*
custard sauce or caramel sauce; ice cream

The Fossoways of the Reach are well-known for producing the best apples in all of Westeros. Their orchards, which sprawl around Cider Hall at the confluence of the Cockleswent and Mander rivers, are the beneficiaries of hundreds of years of skillful cultivation. I had the good fortune to befriend a green-apple Fossoway at the Citadel—a youth from New Barrel, deeply interested in developing novel methods of cultivation. I understood from him that his family was striving to distinguish itself by producing new strains of fruit and exploring previously untried methods of preparation. Upon hearing my enthusiasm for the subject, he shared this family recipe with me.

Yet even without access to Fossoway fruit, this is a winning dessert. The batter for these little crisps fries up light and airy due to the cider and yeast. The frying process transforms crisp autumnal apples into a warm, soft compote while the outside batter stays firm. The crunchiness of the fried batter is enhanced by the sugar coating, and the zest gives a hint of freshness to counter the oil.

½ bottle (6 ounces) sparkling hard cider
A few threads of saffron
Pinch of active dry yeast
Pinch of salt
Zest of ½ lemon or orange

1 cup all-purpose flour
4 medium apples
Coarse sugar, about ¼ cup
Whole cloves, for decoration
Fresh mint leaves, for decoration

➤ **IN A MEDIUM SAUCEPAN,** heat the cider gently over low heat until steaming, then remove from the heat and add the saffron. Allow to sit for about 30 minutes, until the saffron dissolves. Transfer to a medium mixing bowl, stir in the yeast, followed by the salt and zest, and finally add the flour. Beat with a mixer or whisk until the batter is light and smooth and there are no lumps of flour remaining. You should end up with a thick but not unworkable batter. Set aside.

➤ **PEEL THE APPLES.** Using a sharp knife, slice off about ½ inch from the tops of the apples and set aside (once fried, they'll provide a pretty decoration with which to top your reconstructed "fritter-apples"). Core the rest of the apples, then cut them into ½-inch round slices. Pat dry with a paper towel.

➤ **IN A MEDIUM SAUCEPAN** with tall sides, heat about 2 inches of vegetable oil over medium heat to around 365°F; it may take some adjusting to get the temperature just right, especially after you begin frying and some of the oil is absorbed by the fritters. Line a large plate with paper towels, then dip each apple slice (including the apple tops) into the batter before carefully lowering into the hot oil. Let each slice fry for about a minute before gently flipping to cook the other side. The fritters are done when they are golden brown on both sides. Transfer the fried fritters to the plate to drain.

➤ **POUR THE SUGAR** into a shallow bowl. When the slices are all cooked and cool enough to handle, dip them in the sugar.

➤ **TO PRESENT, STACK THE FRITTERS** into the shape of apples (start with a smaller fritter, then stack on a larger fritter followed by a smaller fritter again) and top each stack with one of the fried apple tops. You should hopefully end up with a couple of stacks that loosely resemble apples. If a top has no stem, nestle a clove in the center of the top as a replacement stem, and garnish with a mint leaf to add to the apple impression. These fritters are best served warm.

Cherry Tart

MAKES: *1 tart of about 8 slices*
PREP: *15 minutes*
BAKING: *20 minutes*
PAIRS WELL WITH: *custard sauce or ice cream; Hippocras (page 200)*

When I was a novice, there was a market stall in Oldtown where a sailor-turned-baker sold tarts and pies like those served in the Free City of Lys. I confess, shortly after my arrival at the Citadel, I became enamored of one pastry in particular: a rich cherry tart with a spice blend unlike anything I had ever known. I spent so many afternoons trying to coax the recipe out of the man that I probably could have earned another link had I spent the hours in the library instead, but in the end he relented. The secret lies in the unassuming pit of one particular strain of cherry, imported from Qarth. The seed kernels, extracted from the cherry pit, produce a powerful spice when ground that perfectly complements stone fruits, especially cherries.

The tart itself has a deep, rich flavor, sweetened only by the fruit and a touch of honey. A crisp crust forms the base, while a crumbly, buttery mixture laced with spice reigns above. This tart is equally suited to breakfast or dessert, especially when accompanied by a sweet custard sauce. Although I have never traveled to Lys myself, I can't help believing that there is a touch of those famous Lysene sunsets in each bite of this divine dessert.

2½ pounds fresh cherries, stemmed and
   pitted
¼ cup red wine
Dash of red wine vinegar
½ teaspoon ground cinnamon
¼ teaspoon ground nutmeg
¼ cup honey
1 batch Brown Butter Pastry Crust dough
   (page 22)

TOPPING
½ cup all-purpose flour
¼ cup rolled oats
¼ cup firmly packed brown sugar
2 tablespoons ground almonds
Pinch of salt
2 teaspoons ground mahleb
¼ cup (½ stick) unsalted butter, room
   temperature

➤ PREHEAT THE OVEN to 350°F.

➤ IN A MEDIUM SAUCEPAN, combine the cherries, wine, vinegar, and spices. Set the pan over medium heat and cook until the cherries are quite soft, about 15 minutes. Mash the cherries roughly with a spoon or potato masher, stir in the honey, and transfer to a bowl to cool.

➤ WHILE THE CHERRIES COOL, roll out the pastry dough and gently press it into a standard 9-inch pie pan, trimming off any excess dough. Set aside.

➤ TO MAKE THE TOPPING, combine the flour, oats, brown sugar, ground almonds, salt, and mahleb in a small bowl. Roughly cut in the butter and mash with the other ingredients until the mixture has no butter pieces larger than a pea.

➤ TO ASSEMBLE THE PIE, pour the cooled cherry filling into the lined pie pan. Spread the filling out evenly, then sprinkle the topping over the whole pie, piling a little extra up in the center. Transfer to the oven and bake for about 20 minutes, until the filling is a little bubbly and the crust and topping are a nice golden brown. Allow to cool slightly before slicing.

Honeycake
with Blackberries and Nuts

MAKES: *1 cake of about 8 servings*
PREP: *20 minutes*
BAKING: *20 minutes*
RESTING: *8 hours*
PAIRS WELL WITH: *herbal tea; sweet white wine;*
Pentoshi Honeyed Duck (page 166)

As I was born a Beesbury, I would be remiss to not include a honeycake recipe in this collection. When I was a child, these were one of the most common treats to come out of our kitchen. Indeed, honey was incorporated into nearly every dish on our tables, but this was always one of my favorites. The flavors changed with the seasons and trade, as fruits, spices, and even fresh herbs worked their way through the kitchen gardens and larders.

When baked, the individual layers of this cake are fairly firm—almost like some cookies—but they soften beautifully after the cake is fully assembled, transforming into an almost delicate consistency that is thoroughly enticing to eat. Cut into wedges, the cake's stacked layers make for an elegant presentation. Honey, of course, is at the forefront of the flavors, chased by the more delicate cream and berries, and the slight nuttiness from the outside of the cake.

CAKE
¼ cup (½ stick) unsalted butter, softened
½ cup sugar
1½ teaspoons honey
3 eggs
1 teaspoon baking soda
3½ to 4 cups all-purpose flour

ICING
1 cup heavy cream
½ cup powdered sugar
16 ounces mascarpone, at room temperature
¾ cup blackberries, plus more for garnish
¼ cup walnuts
¼ cup shelled pistachios

➤ **Preheat the oven** to 350°F.

➤ **To make the cake,** beat together the butter and sugar with a hand mixer or spoon in a medium mixing bowl until pale and creamy. Beat in the honey, followed by the eggs, one at a time. Once you have a smooth consistency, stir in the baking soda, then add the flour one cup at a time, until you have a dough that is not too sticky to handle. Turn the dough out onto a floured surface and knead a few times to bring it together. Divide the dough into eight equal balls.

➤ **Working with one ball** at a time, roll out the dough until it is about ¼ inch thick, then cut it into a disc about 6 inches across, using an upside-down bowl or small plate as a template to ensure the rounds are the same size. Place two discs at a time on a baking sheet and bake for about 5 minutes. Repeat until all the dough is used up, baking the scraps for the same amount of time as well.

➤ **To make the icing,** beat the cream using a hand mixer in a medium mixing bowl until it forms soft peaks, just a minute or two. Beat in the powdered sugar, followed by half of the mascarpone and the berries. Fold in the remaining mascarpone with a spoon and set aside.

➤ **In a food processor,** pulse together the walnuts, pistachios, and baked scraps of dough until you have a fairly fine consistency.

➤ **To assemble the cake,** place one of the baked cake layers on a serving plate. Reserve about a third of the icing for frosting the outside of the cake, and set aside. Spread about ¼ cup of the remaining icing over the top of the cake layer, then place another cake layer on top. Repeat until all the cake layers have been incorporated. Spread the reserved third of icing all over the cake, smoothing it out as you go (you may have extra). Using both hands, gently sprinkle and press the nut mixture over the entire cake. Let the cake sit uncovered for at least 8 hours in the fridge to allow the layers to soften.

CHELSEA'S NOTE *The combination of walnuts and pistachios is both flavorful and a colorful contrast to the purple of the berries, but the type of nuts can also be adjusted to suit personal tastes.*

Poppyseed Pastries

MAKES: *6 large pastries*
PREP: *20 minutes*
RISING: *1½ hours*
BAKING: *20 minutes*
PAIRS WELL WITH: *Spiceflower Brew (page 209);*
exotic fresh fruits; sugared nuts

Many Lysene recipes traveled to the Seven Kingdoms during the period known as the Lysene Spring of 135 AC, when Prince Viserys—long feared dead during the Dance of the Dragons—returned from captivity with his Lysene bride. From the writings of Archmaester Gyldayn, we know that this was an enormously prosperous, if brief, period in our history. It ended in a failed coup, the death or flight of most of the Lyseni in King's Landing, and a mistrust of those people and their foreign ways. These pastries fell out of fashion quite soon thereafter—which is a pity, in my estimation, as they are rather unique. I am including them here as a way to reclaim a small part of that lost history, in my own humble way.

My research suggests that the original basis for these pastries may have been Volantene in origin, shaped to resemble fanciful sea dragons of legend. The version that was popular in King's Landing shortly after Prince Viserys's return seems to be almost indistinguishable in ingredients and preparation, though more simply shaped. These delightful whorls are made using the ubiquitous Royal Dough (page 41), combined with a sweetened poppy seed filling. The dough bakes up fluffy and soft, while the filling lends a bit of crunch. These pastries are a fanciful addition to an afternoon tea, as well as a decadent offering for honored guests, although one may wish to consider the sensibilities of those guests before asking the cooks to bake the pastries in the shapes customary in Lys itself.

1 batch Royal Dough (page 41)
1 cup poppy seeds
1 cup almond milk, store-bought or
  homemade (page 44)
1 cup honey or sugar

½ teaspoon ground cardamom
¼ teaspoon ground nutmeg
½ teaspoon pure vanilla extract
Flour, for rolling

➤ WHILE THE DOUGH is rising for the first time, make the poppy seed filling.

➤ GRIND THE POPPY SEEDS in a spice mill, coffee grinder, or by hand in a mortar and pestle, until they look like a fine powder. In a small saucepan over medium heat, combine the ground poppy seeds, milk, honey, and spices. Bring to a simmer and cook for 15 to 20 minutes, until the mixture has thickened appreciably. Remove the pan from the heat and stir in the vanilla. Spread the mixture on a large plate and let it sit for another 30 minutes or so to cool while the dough continues to rise.

➤ WHEN THE DOUGH is ready and the filling has cooled, it's time to form the pastries. Roll out the dough on a lightly floured surface into an approximately 10 by 20-inch rectangle. Spread the filling over the entire piece of dough, making sure the filling reaches all the way to the edges of the rectangle. Starting at one of the long sides of the rectangle, begin rolling the dough into a long log.

➤ TRIM OFF THE ENDS of the log to make them even, then slice the roll into eighteen equal sections about 1 inch thick. Arrange the sections in clusters of three side by side on a baking sheet, ensuring their whorls are all going the same direction.

➤ PREHEAT THE OVEN to 350°F. While the oven preheats, let the slices rise for 20 to 30 minutes, until somewhat puffed. Bake for about 20 minutes, until the pastries have a nice golden color on top. Let cool for a few minutes before enjoying.

Lace Wafer Cookies

MAKES: *About a dozen*
PREP: *15 minutes*
BAKING: *20 minutes*
PAIRS WELL WITH: *Honey Roasted Chickpeas (page 70);*
Spiceflower Brew (page 209)

Although no written record exists that can pinpoint its origin, this ancient recipe may date back to when the Free Cities were young. Both Astapor and Yunkai claim lace wafers as their own, although Astapor's claim is likely the stronger, since the cookies have long been a common offering on the pleasure barges that ply their trade up and down the river called "The Worm," which flows past Astapor. Whatever the case, the knowledge to make these delicate cookies has traveled with the slaves sold around Slaver's Bay, and as a result the cookies are prevalent throughout the area and are even quite common in the Free Cities.

These cookies are wafer thin and a little chewy when still warm from the oven. As they cool, they take on a crisp texture that all but dissolves on the tongue. Earthy tones from the spices and nuts are balanced by a tinge of citrus. The unusual combination of ingredients could only originate somewhere like the western coast of Essos, where trade from both Westeros and the Summer Isles abounds. When the traditional ingredients are not available, other nuts and spices are sometimes swapped in—as was the case with many a regional variety dreamed up by bakers with a penchant for innovation.

½ cup all-purpose flour
⅔ cup shelled pistachios
½ cup raw sugar
1 teaspoon ground cinnamon

¼ cup (½ stick) unsalted/salted butter,
   melted
2 teaspoons lime juice

➤ **PREHEAT THE OVEN** to 300°F and lightly grease a baking sheet with sesame oil.

➤ **COMBINE THE FLOUR,** pistachios, sugar, and cinnamon in a food processor and pulse until the nuts are very fine and no large chunks remain. While pulsing, drizzle in the butter and lime juice, which should bring everything together into a firm dough. If the mixture is still a little dry, a small amount of water can be added. Roll the dough into balls about the size of a walnut, then press flat on the prepared baking sheet to no more than ¼ inch thick. Space these out on the baking sheet and bake for 15 to 20 minutes, until the cookies have turned an even golden brown.

➤ **THE COOKIES WILL KEEP** for several days but are best enjoyed when still slightly warm from the oven.

Fried Fig Tarts

MAKES: *At least a dozen tarts*
PREP: *20 minutes*
FRYING: *20 minutes*
PAIRS WELL WITH: *Hippocras (page 200);*
venison or other game meat

It seems that some version of these tarts has been served at the king's table for at least several hundred years, right up through the reign of our own King Robert. Given their similarity to several dishes common in Essos, these tarts may have traveled to Westeros with the Targaryens, or possibly even earlier with the Andals. In addition to their rich and distinctive flavor, they have the added virtue of versatility. I have seen them adorning the tables of lordly weddings, but they are equally well suited to a lady's private solar, or to the woodland repast of a hunting party.

Whatever the case, these are addictive little morsels—and with good reason. Just small enough to be enjoyed in two or three bites, each tart is stuffed to bursting with spiced figs and honey, then fried until golden. The pastry crisps slightly on the outside, but still retains its chewy softness. The blended spices lend a bite of heat to counterbalance the sweetness of the figs, and a quick basting with honey while the tarts are still warm finishes them to perfection.

8 ounces fresh figs
1 teaspoon Stag's Spice (page 25)
1 tablespoon honey, plus more for basting

1 batch Brown Butter Pastry Crust dough
(page 22)

- FINELY DICE THE FIGS as small as possible by hand, or pulse them in a food processor. Add the diced figs to a small bowl, then mix in the spices and the honey. Set aside.

- ROLL OUT THE DOUGH and cut it into circles about 3 to 4 inches across. On one pastry circle, place a spoonful of figs, brush the edges with a little water, then cover with another circle of dough. Seal the edges well, crimping with the tines of a fork if needed. Repeat this process until all the dough is used up.

- ADD ABOUT ¼ INCH of vegetable oil to a medium saucepan, then set the pan over medium heat. Line a large plate with paper towels, then begin frying the pies in the hot oil until lightly browned and crispy, about 5 minutes, flipping halfway through. Transfer the fried pies to the plate to drain. As soon as the pies have drained, but are still warm, baste them with honey. Eat hot or cold.

MAESTER'S NOTE *If you are making these pies out of season and have only dried figs, soak them in warm water or red wine for a half hour before beginning the recipe. Drain the soaked figs well before using. Some also add crushed nuts, such as walnuts or pistachios, to their tarts, with great success.*

Marzipan

MAKES: *About 2 dozen bites*
PREP: *25 minutes*
DRYING: *About 3 hours*
PAIRS WELL WITH: *dried apricots and nuts;*
Spiced Rum (page 199)

Although hardier branches of almond trees have found a foothold in the more temperate southern regions of Westeros, the sprawling groves of Essos are unrivaled. Less bothered by the harsh winters that plague the north of Westeros, these trees enjoy moderate climate in all seasons, yielding a bountiful harvest for consumption and trade. So great is the demand for almonds in Westeros that many of the ships traveling daily from thence to Pentos are laden with the nuts. Everywhere they are traded they are used in a variety of ways: roasted and candied, or ground with water to create almond milk. Their flour is used in an array of baking and confections, including decorative shapes and subtleties for feasts.

Westerosi recipes for almond paste, as a rule, are less flavorful than those from Pentos or other Free Cities, where they often add a dash of orange blossom water or rose water for a light floral note and a generous pinch of ginger that provides heat on the tongue. Here the almonds are blended with cinnamon, which makes a darker paste and supplies a gentler warmth. With a firm but chewy texture, the paste can be molded into a wide variety of shapes, and is a popular offering for feast days and special occasions. Colors appropriate to the occasion may also be added to match specific sigils, so these small bites are also commonly seen on highborn wedding buffets. I have even heard accounts of garnishes of exotic flowers or gold leaf—a most ostentatious presentation, to be sure.

8 ounces almonds, blanched	**COATING**
1 cup powdered sugar	1 cup powdered sugar, sifted
1 to 2 tablespoons ground cinnamon	Food coloring
2 teaspoons lemon juice	1 to 2 tablespoons almond milk, cow's milk, or water

➤ IN THE BOWL of a food processor, pulse the almonds, powdered sugar, and cinnamon until they reach a very fine consistency. While still pulsing, gradually trickle in the lemon juice. If needed, add a tiny amount of water, a teaspoon or so at a time, until the mixture comes together enough to hold its shape when rolled into a ball.

➤ AT THIS POINT, the mixture can either be rolled out to about ½ inch thick and cut into discs about 2 inches across, or rolled into small balls.

➤ TO MAKE THE COATING, blend the powdered sugar, food coloring, and just enough milk to make a thick icing. Either drizzle the icing over the almond shapes or dip the shapes into the icing, then set the shapes on a cooling rack to let the excess icing drip off. Top with any desired garnishes and let dry completely, at least 2 hours.

Rhoynish Pudding

MAKES: *About 8 servings*
PREP: *10 minutes*
COOKING: *About an hour*
PAIRS WELL WITH: *Lace Wafer Cookies (page 188) or other cookies;*
Winter Tea (page 217)

This unusual pudding has an equally unusual origin. When Princess Nymeria of Ny Sar fled from Essos with her people in their ten thousand ships, they searched for years for a safe harbor in which to build a new home, eventually settling in Dorne. A detail highlighted by Beldecar in his "History of the Rhoynish Wars" is that when Nymeria wed Mors Martell, a huge wedding feast took place, lit by the flames of her ragged fleet. For the feast, the Rhoynar contributed everything they had left from their stores, including an assortment of dried fruit, nuts, grains, and other odd remains collected during their travels. These offerings joined ingredients from the Dornishmen in huge cauldrons, symbolizing in edible form the new unbreakable union between the two peoples.

Although in Dorne this rich dessert is reserved for special occasions and feast days, the orphans of the Greenblood eat it as everyday fare. I have heard tell that a version of this dish has also taken root in Essos, carried thence by the orphans who have returned to the bosom of Mother Rhoyne. The pudding is very sweet, as the Dornish prefer their foods, with a thick base of rice and barley. Added to the mix is an assortment of dried fruits such as currants and apricots, as well as a variety of legumes. It makes for a filling dish equally suited to breakfast as to dessert.

1 cup instant barley

1 cup sugar

One 15-ounce can chickpeas, drained and rinsed

One 15-ounce can navy beans, drained and rinsed

½ cup uncooked white rice

¼ cup currants

2 tablespoons diced dried apricots

2 tablespoons diced dried figs or dates

2 tablespoons pine nuts

2 cinnamon sticks

Pomegranate seeds, to garnish

Shelled pistachios, to garnish

➤ COMBINE THE BARLEY, sugar, chickpeas, beans, rice, currants, apricots, figs, pine nuts, and cinnamon sticks in a large pot and cover with about an inch of water. Cook over medium heat for 1 hour, topping up with water if it looks like there is not enough liquid to keep the ingredients cooking, and stirring often to make sure the pudding doesn't stick to the bottom of the pan. Remove the cinnamon sticks before serving and garnish with pomegranate seeds and pistachios.

Valyrian Gingerbread

MAKES: *About 2 dozen pieces*
COOKING: *10 minutes*
PAIRS WELL WITH: *Hippocras (page 200);*
hot tea; roasted meats

I imagine every highborn person in the Seven Kingdoms is familiar with the lightly spiced dessert that we call gingerbread, but only those as old as I remember the heavier Valyrian version that was popular before the War of the Ninepenny Kings. My research shows that this older recipe has been with us since the conquest, although it was not until the reign of Aegon IV that it became common at royal feasts, where it was often molded into the figures of the current nobility at court. I remember my father telling me of the Valyrian gingerbread served at a feast given by Tytos Lannister when I was scarcely a boy; it made an impression. Steady-handed cooks and a bevy of nervous apprentices had gilded gingerbread beasts with the purest gold of Casterly Rock, beaten so thin that the slightest breath sent bright flakes fluttering away before each bite. No doubt it was this memory that led me to search out this particular recipe for inclusion.

Although I do love the gingerbread that's popular now, this earlier recipe is oddly enticing. It makes for a gingerbread that's dense and warm and chewy, and best served in sparing quantity, as it has a much more intense spice profile than the more familiar version. I have found it pairs well with hot drinks, especially mulled wine, and I like to think that one or two of these slim treats aid greatly in digestion: the ideal capstone to a monumental meal.

½ cup honey
¼ cup red wine
1 teaspoon ground ginger
½ teaspoon ground cinnamon

Pinch of ground black pepper
Pinch of ground anise
1 cup plain bread crumbs

➥ COMBINE THE HONEY, red wine, and spices in a small saucepan over medium heat. Once the honey and wine have combined, stir in the bread crumbs. Continue stirring until the mixture has stiffened and pulls away from the sides of the pan. Remove the pan from the heat and transfer the dough to a silicone mat or a sheet of parchment paper. Lay another mat or sheet of parchment paper on top of the dough, and roll it out while still warm, ¼ inch to ½ inch thick. Cut the dough into diamonds or other desired shapes. The gingerbread is good enjoyed warm, but may be spread out on a silicone pad or parchment paper and allowed to dry for several days.

MAESTER'S NOTE *For a darker, fruitier version, substitute half of the honey for pomegranate molasses. Also, if you wish to gild the gingerbread in the manner of previous reigns, simply use clean painter's brushes to apply thin sheets of pure beaten gold leaf while the gingerbread pieces are still sticky on top. Allow the gilded gingerbread to dry as above.*

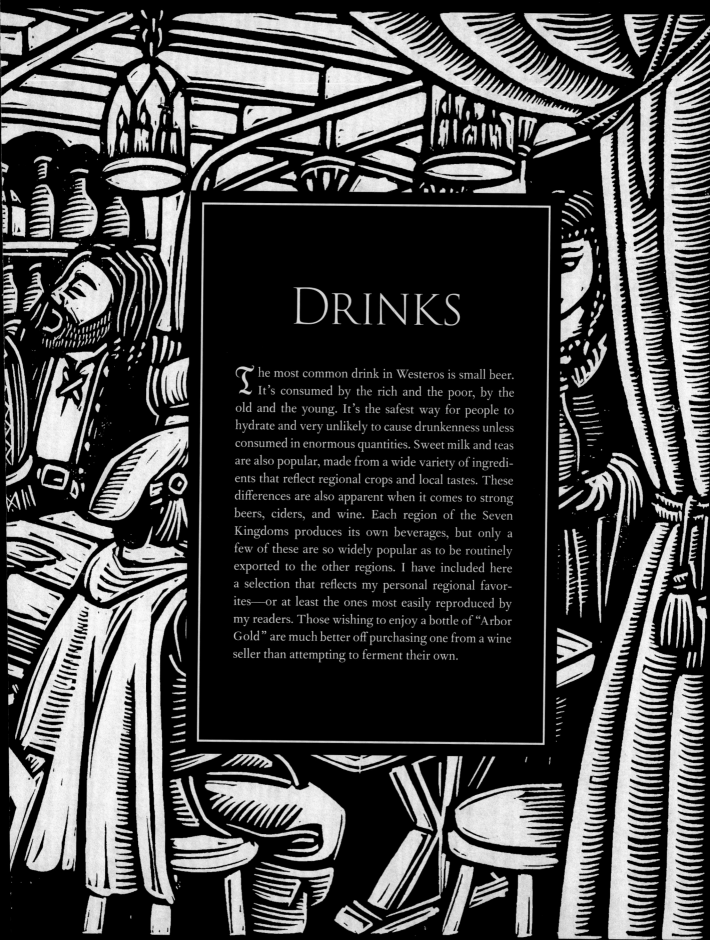

DRINKS

T he most common drink in Westeros is small beer. It's consumed by the rich and the poor, by the old and the young. It's the safest way for people to hydrate and very unlikely to cause drunkenness unless consumed in enormous quantities. Sweet milk and teas are also popular, made from a wide variety of ingredients that reflect regional crops and local tastes. These differences are also apparent when it comes to strong beers, ciders, and wine. Each region of the Seven Kingdoms produces its own beverages, but only a few of these are so widely popular as to be routinely exported to the other regions. I have included here a selection that reflects my personal regional favorites—or at least the ones most easily reproduced by my readers. Those wishing to enjoy a bottle of "Arbor Gold" are much better off purchasing one from a wine seller than attempting to ferment their own.

Spiced Rum
as from the Summer Isles

MAKES: *750 milliliters, about 6 servings*
PREP: *5 minutes*
STEEPING: *1 week to 2 months*
PAIRS WELL WITH: *Honey Roasted Chickpeas (page 70);*
spicy Dornish dishes

The Summer Isles are famed for their spiced rum, the taste of which evokes warm sands, long sunny days, and fresh breezes off the water. Although I have not been to the Isles myself, I learned a great deal in conversation with sailors and sea captains whose livelihoods depend on voyages to and from that southern archipelago. They tell me that in Tall Trees Town, rum is distilled from sugarcane and aged in charred oak casks for at least eight years, while on at least one of the southernmost islands, the honey of a small stingless bee is used to produce the liquor, and the aging process is complete after only three years. Exotic spices and fruits are added in, along with a vanilla bean, and allowed to infuse with the spirits until the whole beverage is a rich golden color and smells of citrus. Although we tend to think of such rum as a single spirit, the truth is that these rums are likely as varied and distinct as the Summer Islanders themselves.

The recipe included below is the result of much trial and error on my part, as I have never directly witnessed the rum's production. And although it cannot compare with the true rum from the Summer Isles, it conveys a strong sense of the original, I hope. The initial impression of this rum is sharp and warm, with a sweetness on the tongue that's chased by a pleasant burn of spice.

One 750-milliliter bottle medium-bodied
  aged rum
3 allspice berries
3 whole cloves
1 cardamom pod
1 cinnamon stick

⅛ teaspoon grated nutmeg
5 strips of orange peel, 4 to 5 inches long,
  white pith removed
½ vanilla bean, seeds scraped
¼ cup raw sugar or honey

➤ POUR OUT ABOUT ⅓ CUP of the rum from the bottle and reserve for another use, or discard. Add the remaining ingredients to the bottle and reseal with the cap. Place the bottle in a dark spot for at least a week, shaking every few days. Strain into a clean bottle when ready to enjoy. This rum will keep indefinitely at room temperature.

Hippocras

MAKES: *750 milliliters, about 6 servings*
PREP: *About 30 minutes*
INFUSING: *1 to 3 days*
PAIRS WELL WITH: *rich red meat; Cherry Tart (page 178)*

According to Maester Gyldayn's "Fire and Blood," hippocras may have arrived in Westeros along with the Targaryens. However, the original concept—one of spices steeped in sweetened wine—is likely considerably older. Indeed, several fragments of medical texts from Essos include instructions for making similar beverages, which were prized for their ability to balance the humors. Given the expensive spice profile of the ingredients, these so-called remedies would have been accessible only to the wealthy—even in Essos, where such spices are more readily available.

Even if originally intended only as a medicinal cordial, hippocras has since grown in popularity as a digestif following a rich meal or a nightcap before bed. I have found that it imparts a feeling of well-being that radiates from the center of the chest outwards. The flavor is quite sweet, with a sharp bite of spices at the fore and a more mellow, pleasant burn that lingers on the tongue. A small glass of fortified hippocras is generally sufficient to warm the bones, although there are some who have been known to quaff it. Such indulgence is ill-advised, and invariably leads to the mightiest of headaches the following morning.

*One 750-milliliter bottle red wine, such as
  Bordeaux*
½ cup sugar, or more to taste
2 teaspoons ground ginger
1 teaspoon whole cloves
½ teaspoon caraway seed

½ teaspoon dried galangal
½ teaspoon ground nutmeg
½ teaspoon ground grains of paradise
½ teaspoon ground long pepper
3 cinnamon sticks

➥ COMBINE ALL THE INGREDIENTS in a medium pot over medium heat. Heat the wine until it is steaming and the sugar has dissolved, then remove from the heat. Let the wine sit on the spices at room temperature for at least 24 hours, or up to 3 days, then taste and adjust sweetness as desired. Strain the wine several times through fine mesh until it runs clear, then pour into a clean bottle. Cap and store somewhere dark for up to 2 weeks, or several months if fortified as below.

➥ FOR A MORE ROBUST VERSION, this recipe can be fortified with the addition of 1 cup of brandy, and served in small glasses.

Kvass

MAKES: *½ gallon*
PREP: *15 minutes*
FERMENTING: *3 days (or longer)*
PAIRS WELL WITH: *Onion Broth with Carrot and Goat (page 94);*
rustic bread

Only those who have visited the Wall in winter can appreciate the awful cruelty of a wind that tears the breath from a man's lungs and howls over the naked spine of the North like something out of those stories rangers tell around hearth fires in the bowels of Castle Black. In such an environment, men must take whatever nourishment they can, and absolutely nothing can be wasted. A steward I spoke to during my visit early in the fifth year of King Robert's reign explained how stale bread is incorporated into stews or drinks, and only the most inedible scraps go to the livestock. The drink I have included here is curiously similar to one Maester Willis recounts being consumed by the wildlings in his text "Hardhome," so it is possible the technique originated with them and was learned by the black brothers, whose dealings with the free folk, as they call themselves, are more nuanced than most of us understand.

In any case, this drink is a perfect example of the ingenuity of the stewards of the Night's Watch (though the stewards are said to cook and prepare meals, there is a head cook at Castle Black: Three-Finger Hobb). It incorporates stale bread, the most hearty of weedy mint that thrives even in the North, and apples, either dried in winter or shredded when fresh from orchards in the Gift. The flavor is mild yet nourishing, with traces of the apple and mint, but rye-forward. A slight fizz makes it a refreshing chaser to the often heavy foods that come out of the kitchens in Castle Black. Indeed, it is so preferred to water that flagons of the stuff are served at most meals, sometimes chilled with a chip of ice.

1 pound heavy rye bread
1 apple, cored and shredded
2 to 3 sprigs mint
8 cups boiling water

1 cup honey
1 teaspoon brewer's yeast or baker's yeast
7 raisins

➤ TEAR THE BREAD into pieces, then put the pieces in a large saucepot along with the apple and mint. Pour the boiling water into the pot, cover, and allow to sit at room temperature for about 2 hours, until cooled but still a little warm.

➤ STRAIN THE MIXTURE into a large glass jar and add the honey, yeast, and raisins. Top with a fermenting airlock and allow to work for about 3 days. When the raisins are dancing about in the liquid, it's ready to enjoy.

MAESTER'S NOTE *A little grated or ground ginger can be added along with the yeast when available, and/or Rosehip Syrup (page 30). Sourdough starter may also be used in place of the yeast. And while the black brothers drink this brew cloudy, swimming with bits of bread, others may prefer it strained a few times for a clearer pour.*

Mead
Three Ways

MAKES: *1 gallon*
PREP: *30 minutes*
FERMENTING: *2 months (or longer)*
PAIRS WELL WITH: *Tenderloin Skewers (page 165);*
Honeycake with Blackberries and Nuts (page 180)

As any maester with a silver link can attest, the line between food and healing is fluid—and in this case, quite literally. As a child, I remember the litany of meads produced at our family estates: magical sounding words—pyment, cyser, metheglin, rhodomel, braggot, melomel—all describing the wondrous combination of our honey with an array of other ingredients, each of which is said to have special benefits to the health of the body. I must confess, however, that in my own studies, I have been less interested in the healing properties of honey wine and more intrigued by variations on traditional brewing methods. I have even seen some text in a scrap of an epic poem alluding to a potion made from the fermented sap of a wierwood tree, just as birch sap is sometimes added to mead in the Neck.

Included here is a basic mead recipe that uses the same standard proportions as nearly every batch I helped brew in my youth, along with three variations. The flavor of mead is highly malleable depending on the season in which the honey is harvested and the other ingredients incorporated, but this recipe in all its iterations allows much of the honey's natural sweetness to remain. It is not so strong as the meads generally found in the North, which are often fortified to keep them from freezing. That said, I have created my own version of a northern mead, inspired by the spice profile of the meals I enjoyed during a visit to Winterfell in the days of Aerys II Targaryen. Also included are a melomel brewed with fresh seasonal fruit, and an herbal metheglin that contains several ingredients known by the Citadel to promote healing.

10 cups water
Regional fruits, herbs, or spices, optional
   (see below)
4 cups (about 3 pounds) honey
1 heaping tablespoon roughly chopped
   raisins
1 packet ale yeast

SPECIAL EQUIPMENT
1-gallon glass jug
Brewing airlock and plug
Funnel

recipe continues

➤ BEGIN BY CAREFULLY WASHING all the equipment in boiling water and rinsing each of them thoroughly.

➤ BOIL HALF OF THE WATER in a large pot, then remove the pot from the heat. Add any desired regional fruits, herbs, or spices, then stir in the honey until dissolved. Carefully pour the hot mixture, spices and all, into the glass jug using a funnel. Add the remaining water and allow the mixture to cool for several hours, until just a little warmer than room temperature.

➤ ADD THE RAISINS AND YEAST to the jug, then seal the jug with the plug and fermentation airlock. In several hours, the airlock should be bubbling—a good indicator that fermentation has begun. Allow the beverage to ferment at room temperature in a dark place for at least 1 month, but ideally 2 months. The mead will increase in potency the longer it ferments, from a little fizzy and quite sweet at the fore to stronger and less sweet as time goes on. Taste your brew periodically every few days or weeks, replacing the airlock afterward, and when it is to your liking, serve it up.

➤ TO ENJOY, STRAIN THE MEAD through a filter and either serve straightaway or bottle with all proper precautions. There are many texts available that go into considerably more depth about the practicalities of bottling, and I heartily recommend reading some of those if you intend to bottle and age your mead.

MAESTER'S NOTE *It is of paramount importance that you let the mead ferment completely before bottling. If not, pressure may continue to build inside the sealed bottles, and with nowhere to go, explosions are possible. I discovered this firsthand when I attempted to brew a new recipe in secret as a gift for my aunt Ellyn, which resulted in crockery shards everywhere and blueberry stains that may yet be visible on the cellar ceiling.*

Additional Ingredients for Metheglin

3 tablespoons fresh herbs (such as lemon balm, angelica, thyme,
hyssop, agrimony, meadowsweet)
1 tablespoon fresh strong herbs (such as mint, rosemary, sage, etc.)
2 tablespoons freshly grated ginger
10 whole cloves
2 cinnamon sticks

Additional Ingredients for Southern Melomel

1 cup fresh fruit, roughly chopped or mashed
1 teaspoon freshly grated ginger

Additional Ingredients for Northern Mead

1½ teaspoons coriander seed
1½ teaspoons juniper berries
1½ teaspoons crushed cinnamon sticks

Spiceflower Brew

MAKES: *2 servings*
COOKING: *10 minutes*
PAIRS WELL WITH: *Creamy Chestnut Soup (page 100);*
Lace Wafer Cookies (page 188)

Spiceflower is little known in Westeros except perhaps to maesters seeking to deepen their knowledge of herblore. This is likely due to the plant's relative rarity, as spiceflower grows only in the Dothraki sea in Essos. Its suggestively shaped roots are topped by tall spikes of purple flowers that grow along the edges of the sea, where the immensely tall grasses begin to give way to other plants. The fresh blooms make a heady perfume, while the roots are ground into a powder for culinary uses, such as this Braavosi beverage. Giant brass urns of the drink simmer over hot coals throughout the winter in Braavos, leaving the air redolent with the scent of cinnamon and spice. It wards off the chill of the canals, and is an immensely popular drink in the cold seasons when its sudden appearance in market stalls softens the blow of winter's arrival. In addition, many Braavosi believe that spiceflower possesses aphrodisiac qualities, perhaps because of the root's suggestive shape.

It has been many years since I have crossed the narrow sea myself, but last spring a colleague of mine brought some powdered spiceflower to the Citadel and was kind enough to share. I must say, the taste is incomparable—just as I remembered from my youth. The resultant brew is thick, unusually flavorful, and warming down to the bones. I'm told that some shops add a pinch of Lyseni mastic to the pot, which gives the drink a subtle piney flavor not unlike juniper in the north of Westeros. Other shops add a pinch of costly saffron, which imparts a yellow hue and adds complexity to the flavor.

2½ cups almond milk, store-bought or
* homemade (page 44)*
2½ teaspoons powdered arrowroot
Pinch of ground nutmeg, plus more for
* garnish*
Pinch of ground ginger

Pinch of ground cinnamon, plus more for
* garnish*
2 tablespoons sugar, or to taste
Pinch of ground mastic and/or ground
* saffron, ground together with the sugar,*
* if desired*

➤➤ WHISK ALL THE INGREDIENTS together in a medium saucepan over medium heat. While whisking, heat the milk until it is steaming, but stop just shy of boiling it. Continue to cook until the mixture thickens noticeably, several minutes. Strain the brew into two clean heatproof mugs and garnish with an extra pinch of ground cinnamon and nutmeg. Serve hot.

Myrish Firewine

MAKES: *750 milliliters, about 6 servings*
PREP: *5 minutes*
COOKING: *20 minutes*
PAIRS WELL WITH: *Dragonstone Jaerhilla (page 97);*
Roast Goose Sauced with Mulberries (page 152)

The prized ingredient in this wine is mastic, an unassuming little dollop of hardened resin that is highly valued for its flavor and medicinal qualities. The trees that produce this precious sap grow only on the isles surrounding Lys, and the harvesting process is laborious. The trees are scored until they weep, and the drops of hardened resin are carefully collected from a bed of powdered clay into which they drip. After carefully aging in dark warehouses, the "tears," as these drops of resin are called, are sorted according to size and purity. They can be ground with salt or sugar for easier inclusion in a variety of recipes, and are even used in some cosmetic preparations in Lys. It is worth noting that while there is no culinary relation between this resin and the so-called tears of Lys, their similarity in name may shed some light on the production of that infamous poison. But that is an undertaking for a different maester than I.

The wine has a color ranging from light golden to a darker amber. The flavor is round, with a thick honey-sweetness that's followed by the slow burn of pepper on the tip of the tongue. The bite of mastic cuts through what could otherwise only be called cloying, while the anise flavor itself is more subtle, imparting a warming nature to the wine through its aroma and taste. Nonetheless, I advise cutting the mixture with a little water to taste, as is the custom in Lys. In other cities where the wine is imported, it is sometimes fortified with brandy or other strong spirits for long sea voyages, or added to juice or other wine as a flavoring. A less popular variant pairs this recipe with a red wine and cinnamon sticks, although this is so reminiscent of our own mulled wine as to seem lackluster.

One 750-milliliter bottle white wine
1 cup honey
1 Medjool date, pitted and diced
1 teaspoon ground black pepper

½ teaspoon finely ground mastic gum
Pinch of finely ground saffron
2 bay leaves

➤ COMBINE 1 CUP OF THE WINE with the honey in a small saucepan and bring to a boil. Once the honey has dissolved, reduce the heat to a simmer and add the remaining ingredients. Let the mixture simmer for about 10 minutes, then remove it from the heat and allow it to sit for another 10 minutes. Add the remaining wine, then pour everything through a fine sieve into a clean bottle. You may need to strain the liquid more than once to achieve a clear appearance.

➤ TO SERVE, MIX TO TASTE with water, either hot or cold, in a ratio of about one-to-one.

Volantene Ale

MAKES: *2 servings*
PREP: *10 minutes*
STEEPING: *2 hours (or longer)*
PAIRS WELL WITH: *Crown Roast of Boar's Ribs (page 157);*
Valyrian Gingerbread (page 195)

The inhabitants of Volantis are known for their collective sweet tooth, so it seems only natural they would extend that preference to their libations as well. The drought-resistant sugar beets of the region thrive despite the sweltering climate. The beets themselves are often made directly into rich dishes, such as the famed sweet Volantene beet soup, but are also refined into sugar for export to other cities surrounding Slaver's Bay. The quality of the sugar depends upon the length of refinement: the finest sugars retain only the slightest pink color, while the rest range from dark purple to a middling vermilion hue.

It is this midrange sugar that is usually used for this recipe everywhere except for the ports, where residual beet flavor is not considered undesirable, especially by the less discerning sailors. The addition of a sweetened fruit syrup enlivens just about any beer, no matter the quality. Perhaps it was Volantene sailors who first discovered this trick with their kegs of beer meant for long sea voyages, or an enterprising tavern owner with an overabundance of fruit on the edge of spoiling. Whatever the case, the resulting beverage is cool from the cellar-chilled ale and sweet on the tongue, making it a popular means throughout the city to beat the oppressive summer heat. The varieties are limited only by the harvest and availability of specialty ales. Some establishments are even known to add a dash of spirits, such as Myrish Firewine (page 210), to increase the beverage's potency.

¼ cup sugar
¼ cup water
1 apple, cored and diced

½ cup hulled and sliced strawberries
½ cup raspberries
2 pints chilled amber ale

➤ COMBINE THE SUGAR AND WATER in a small saucepan over medium heat, swirling occasionally until the sugar has dissolved. Remove from the heat and allow to cool slightly. Place the fruit in a medium bowl and pour the sugar syrup over it. Cover and let this sit for at least 2 hours at room temperature, or overnight in the fridge for a stronger flavor.

➤ TO SERVE, DIVIDE THE FRUIT SYRUP between two tall glasses and top with the beer.

Winter Town Wassail

MAKES: *About 10 servings*
PREP: *10 minutes*
COOKING: *30 minutes*
PAIRS WELL WITH: *roasted meats such as venison;*
Apple Crisps (page 176)

Those who have traveled little in the North may not know of the winter town; it's the name given to the settlement that huddles in the shadow of Winterfell. It's mostly abandoned in the warmer seasons, but as the falling autumn leaves mingle with the first snows, the town springs to life as smallfolk stream into the squat log houses that offer a safe refuge and place of community for northerners who would otherwise be left isolated by the deep snows. Farmers load their harvests into wagons and drive the last of their livestock before them, and when they arrive, there is a celebration which involves a beverage they call the wassail.

This hot, fortifying drink is especially popular in the spacious inn aptly named the Smoking Log for its fires that never go out. Steaming cauldrons of the brew are set atop coals outside the front door, where patrons and passersby may purchase a mug-full for a few pennies. The predominant flavor of this wassail is of spiced cider, often of apples and pears, which largely masks the addition of fortifying spirits. This brew has proved the undoing of many a green youth still new to the town, but I was thankfully forewarned that it is intended as a bracing drink to warm against the winter chill rather than something to be quaffed in great quantity. Indeed, from what I was given to understand, wassail is unforgiving to those who make it the centerpiece of a night of indulgence.

1 gallon non-alcoholic apple or pear cider

One 12-ounce bottle ale

1½ cups dry sherry

½ cup brandy

½ cup maple syrup

½ cup whiskey or bourbon

3 cinnamon sticks

1 tablespoon juniper berries

2 apples, cored and diced

➥ COMBINE ALL THE INGREDIENTS in a large pot over medium-low heat (the apple slices will float in the mixture as it warms gently). Keep the mixture below a simmer for around 30 minutes. When it's steaming, it's ready to serve.

MAESTER'S NOTE *Holiday ales with notes of cloves and other spices are generally best for this recipe. If you like, you can double the level of alcohol without compromising the wonderful way the flavors all meld together. Also, for an interesting varietal, try steeping a few sprigs of thyme in the mixture while it warms. This produces a slightly more medicinal flavor, but in a very good way.*

Winter Tea

MAKES: *2 servings*
PREP: *5 minutes*
STEEPING: *5 minutes*
PAIRS WELL WITH: *Honeycake with Blackberries and Nuts (page 180);*
lighter meals

Herblore, especially in service to the healing arts, is one of the most important fields of study for every acolyte at the Citadel. No matter the eventual posting a maester might receive, he can be sure that he will be called upon for his healing skills, even in times of peace. And in many cases, attending to the health of one's charges is as much about preventing illness as about curing it. Especially in the long winter months, when good nutrition becomes increasingly hard to achieve, a maester must know tinctures, brews, and extracts that will promote good health amongst those he serves. Winter tea is one such wholesome infusion.

The recipe for this tea was taught to me by Maester Gerard, who asserted that each of the tea's ingredients has a beneficial quality. He and many other maesters have observed a certain winter sickness, prevalent especially in the North, that yields symptoms like loosened teeth and, in the worst instances, the reopening of old wounds. This affliction can be easily avoided, however, with a small amount of this preparation, consumed regularly. The flavor of the recipe as written is subtly herbal, with light citrus notes and a little acidic bite from the vinegar.

1 bag of nettle or chamomile tea
½ teaspoon dried orange, lime, or lemon
peel, finely chopped
1 tablespoon dried fruit (such as elderberry,
apple, or apricot)

Splash of cider vinegar
Rosehip Syrup (page 30), or 1 tablespoon
dried rosehips
Honey to sweeten (optional)

➤ COMBINE THE TEA, citrus peel, dried fruit, vinegar, and Rosehip Syrup in a heatproof mug, then pour boiling water into the mug and allow the tea to steep for about 5 minutes before straining. Sweeten with the honey to taste. The mixture can be used to make a second cup of tea, as well.

MAESTER'S NOTE *Other useful additions, when available, are young white pine needles, violet leaves, thyme, ginger, etc. Anything that thrives in spring and summer and has been suitably preserved is a welcome addition to this heartening brew.*

Dothraki Pepper Beer Syrup

MAKES: *About 4 servings*
PREP: *5 minutes*
COOKING: *10 minutes*
PAIRS WELL WITH: *Dothraki Blood Pies (page 143); roasted meats*

The practice of gifting is deeply ingrained within the culture of the Dothraki, who consider the buying and selling of goods to be largely disgraceful. The Dothraki are glad to accept gifts from some of the Free Cities—who, in turn, receive the "gift" of the Dothraki khalasar's departure from their gates. Not infrequently, these gifts take the form of provisions, such as beer, grain, meat, fresh fruit, or spices. These, as well as the spoils from looting, are immediately put to use feeding the khalasar. Some have noted that lords of the Free Cities often try to pass off lower quality beer to their Dothraki visitors, and this peppery syrup is the clever answer to such a problem. Any middling-quality beer can be greatly improved by the addition of such a syrup as this, which masks the true flavor of the beer with strong spices.

The slight peppery sensation builds over time to a lingering burn that fills the mouth in a not entirely unpleasant way. The layered peppers provide a small but bright burst of flavor near the front of the tongue, which then rounds out the whole sip of beer with a deeper and more complex flavor. The slight numbing quality of some pepper varieties included here may also account for this recipe's success at making poor beer more palatable.

2 tablespoons jaggery or raw sugar
1 cup vodka
½ teaspoon ground black pepper

1 tablespoon ground Szechuan peppercorns
3 teaspoons ground grains of paradise
5 whole star anise

➤ COMBINE ALL THE INGREDIENTS in a jar, then seal and let stand at room temperature, shaking every few hours, for at least a day (though the flavors will grow stronger over time). When ready to serve, strain the syrup through a very fine sieve into a clean bottle.

➤ TO USE, add roughly 3 tablespoons of the syrup to 12 ounces of your beer of choice.

Dōnor Vīgilla

MAKES: *About 4 servings*
COOKING: *5 minutes*
CHILLING: *30 minutes*
PAIRS WELL WITH: *spicy Dornish dishes, such as Spicy Lentil Stew (page 99);*
Honey Roasted Chickpeas (page 70)

Dōnor Vīgilla is a refreshing beverage often used to fortify oneself against sun and heat. It's made by combining vinegar, sugar or honey, and other fruits and herbs to create a cordial that is then diluted with water. In addition to its satisfying flavor, it is prized for practical reasons, as the undiluted mixture can keep indefinitely. Aboard ships, it's used to improve the flavor of stale water and prevent sea-born illnesses, while in Dorne, flasks of the stuff are stowed away in saddlebags for long journeys across the desert. Throughout the lordly houses of southern Westeros, Dōnor Vīgilla is a popular refreshment in hot weather, and some maesters have even argued the drink helps to combat the wasting sickness that affects so many in the North during Westeros's long winters.

Although many variations of this beverage exist, all have a common ancestor in the Old Ghiscari Empire. From there, the drink seems to have spread throughout the known world. The Andals had a version with cider vinegar, honey, and dried native berries, while the dragonlords of Old Valyria had a sweeter honeyed concoction with exotic spices and herbs, some of which are now lost to time and the tides. Nowadays, the drink can be found everywhere from Lannisport to Lys. The Dornish incarnation features blood orange and fiery peppers, but my favorite variation is one I encountered during a lazy summer in the Reach. There, some of the most flavorful berries are reduced into a thick syrup, then flavored and garnished with mint. Served alongside pitchers of water and chips of ice, this sweet cordial can be diluted to suit individual tastes and fortify guests against the sweltering summer heat.

½ cup red wine vinegar   *1 cup sugar*

➤ COMBINE THE VINEGAR AND SUGAR in a medium saucepan and simmer for around 5 minutes, until the sugar is dissolved. Let the syrup cool, then when ready to serve, dilute it in cold or hot water using a one-to-three ratio.

MAESTER'S NOTES *Other ingredients can be added to the syrup once the sugar has dissolved. To add fresh fruit, boil the fruit with a little water in a separate pan, mashing the fruit periodically until you have a thick juice, then strain the liquid into a clean vessel before adding it to the vinegar mixture. Alternatively, you can steep whole spices in the hot sugar mixture until it cools, then strain before serving.*

If adding other ingredients to the syrup—especially fresh fruit—it's best to keep the mixture chilled until use, up to 3 weeks.

Dishes Organized by Region

All of Westeros

Bread and Salt
Sigil Bread
Fried Breadsticks

The North

Rosehip Syrup
Oaten Porridge with Cheese
Pease Pie Laced with Bacon
Mead
Winter Tea
Garlic Sausage Patties
Barley Griddlecakes
Beef and Barley Soup

WHITE HARBOR

White Harbor Meat Pie

THE WALL

Onion Broth with Carrot and Goat
Kvass
Salted Cod Cakes

WINTERFELL

*Mutton Chops Sauced with
Honey and Spice*
Winter Town Wassail

The South

Mustard from Oldtown
Royal Dough
Seasoned Butter
Mead
*Thick Cream of Wheat with Honey
and Butter*
Fried Fig Tarts
Valyrian Gingerbread
Roast Goose Sauced with Mulberries
Boiled Beef with Horseradish Sauce
Boiled Beans with Bacon
Pottage with Spring Greens

STORMLANDS

*Garlic Broth with Chunks of Whitefish,
Carrot, and Onion*

RIVERLANDS

Potted Hare
Riverlands Creamed Leeks

THE REACH

Poor Knights
Highgarden Dumplings
Stewed Plums
Apple Crisps
Honeycake with Blackberries and Nuts
Gravy-Poached Eggs
Redwyne Roasted Grapes
*Dressed Greens with Apples
and Pine Nuts*

IRON ISLANDS

Ironborn Ship's Biscuits

DRAGONSTONE, STEPSTONES
Dragonstone Jaerhilla
Stargazy Pie
Mango Relish

KING'S LANDING
Crown Roast of Boar's Ribs
Hippocras
Almond Milk
Marzipan
Creamy Chestnut Soup
Sesame Rings
Cinnamon Swirled Loaf

DORNE
Dōnor Vīgilla
Rhoynish Pudding
Honey Roasted Chickpeas
Dornish Roasted Red Pepper Paste

ACROSS THE NARROW SEA IN ESSOS
Klihilla Sauce
Spice Blends from Old Ghis and the Freehold
Mango Relish
Jaedo Havon

SUMMER ISLES
Spiced Rum

DOTHRAKI
Dothraki Pepper Beer Syrup
Dothraki Blood Pies
Dothraki Dahanikh

BRAAVOS
Braavosi Pepperfish
Spiceflower Brew
Braavosi Mussels
Fried Pepper Sardines
Olive Loaf

VOLANTIS
Volantene Ale

PENTOS
Pentoshi Curried Mushrooms
Pentoshi Buttered Parsnips
Egg-Lemon Soup
Pentoshi Honeyed Duck

LYS
Poppyseed Pastries
Cherry Tart

ASTAPOR
Lace Wafer Cookies

MEEREEN
Meereenese Soup with Ginger
Flaky Flatbread

MYR
Firewine

Suggested Menus

A Day in the North

Barley Griddlecakes with Rosehip Syrup
Oaten Porridge with Cheese
Garlic Sausage Patties

Onion Broth with Carrot and Goat
Fried Breadsticks
Salted Cod Cakes

Pease Pie Laced with Bacon
Mutton Chops Sauced with Honey and Spice
Stewed Plums
Mead or Winter Town Wassail

A Day in the South

Poor Knights with Rosehip Syrup
Winter Tea

Redwyne Roasted Grapes
Cheeses and Candied Nuts
Pottage with Spring Greens

Crown Roast of Boar's Ribs
Highgarden Dumplings
Marzipan or Valyrian Gingerbread

A Journey up the King's Road

Thick Cream of Wheat with Honey and Butter
Toasted Cinnamon Swirled Loaf with Seasoned Butter

Boiled Beans with Bacon
Beef and Barley Soup
Sigil Bread

White Harbor Meat Pie
Riverlands Creamed Leeks
Mead

Sailing Around Westeros

Mango Relish
Ironborn Ship's Biscuits
Garlic Broth with Chunks of Whitefish, Carrot, and Onion

Feasting in the Free Cities

Dothraki Dahanikh
Exotic Fruits

Meereenese Soup with Ginger
Flaky Flatbread

Braavosi Mussels with Jaedo Havon
Pentoshi Honeyed Duck and Buttered Parsnips
Lace Wafer Cookies
Myrish Firewine

Acknowledgments

The greatest compiled knowledge in the Citadel results from the labors of countless maesters, scholars, and seekers of knowledge and truth. Indeed, this work in your hands could not exist without the labor of many others. From the bakers of Braavos to the dauntless cooks who feed the entire Red Keep, those who have aided my efforts are too numerous to count, but I would be remiss to not recognize these particular few below.

Bregowine Bracken, a scholar, whose considerable support and keen literary eye have provided the firm foundation on which all my efforts are built.

Archmaester Dedalus, who helped enormously with the translation of the more obscure texts I encountered throughout the course of my research.

Big Jon Cassel for his warm smile, endless encouragement, and hearty appetite, and Maggy the Builder for her tireless efforts on my behalf. Also Mistress Kate, for her quiet help in the kitchen and wrangling my novices.

Lastly, my young novices, Pip and Rafe, for their careful study of all I could teach them, as well as their considered rebuttals at times. May their inquiring minds continue to search for truths and culinary innovations.

—Chelsea Monroe-Cassel

Index

About the Authors

Chelsea Monroe-Cassel is a lifelong artist and fan of both fantasy and food. Like the literature she loves, each of Chelsea's cookbooks is a synthesis of imagination and historical research that brings a fantastical world to life. Her immersive work has received rave reviews from fans and critics alike for its ability to extend fandoms into real-world kitchens. She is the author of nine bestselling cookbooks, including *A Feast of Ice and Fire: The Official Game of Thrones Companion Cookbook*, *World of Warcraft: The Official Cookbook*, *The Star Trek Cookbook*, *Star Wars—Galaxy's Edge: The Official Black Spire Outpost Cookbook*, *Firefly: The Big Damn Cookbook*, and *The Elder Scrolls: The Official Cookbook*. Chelsea lives in Vermont with her family, her cats, and about seven pounds of bees.

George R. R. Martin is the #1 *New York Times* bestselling author of many novels, including those of the acclaimed series A Song of Ice and Fire—*A Game of Thrones*, *A Clash of Kings*, *A Storm of Swords*, *A Feast for Crows*, and *A Dance with Dragons*—as well as related works such as *Fire & Blood*, *A Knight of the Seven Kingdoms*, *The World of Ice & Fire*, and *Rise of the Dragon* (the last two with Elio M. García, Jr., and Linda Antonsson). Other novels and collections include *Tuf Voyaging*, *Fevre Dream*, *The Armageddon Rag*, *Dying of the Light*, *Windhaven* (with Lisa Tuttle), and *Dreamsongs, Volumes I* and *II*. As a writer-producer, he has worked on *The Twilight Zone*, *Beauty and the Beast*, and various feature films and pilots that were never made. He lives with his lovely wife, Parris, in Santa Fe, New Mexico.

Text copyright © 2024 by CHELSEA MONROE-CASSEL
Foreword copyright © 2024 by GEORGE R. R. MARTIN
Photographs copyright © 2024 by LAUREN VOLO
Illustrations copyright © 2024 by BRIAN REEDY

Published in the United States by RANDOM HOUSE WORLDS, an imprint of RANDOM HOUSE, a division of PENGUIN RANDOM HOUSE LLC, New York.
RandomHouseBooks.com

RANDOM HOUSE is a registered trademark, and RANDOM HOUSE WORLDS and colophon are trademarks of PENGUIN RANDOM HOUSE LLC.

Hardcover ISBN 978-0-593-59945-7
Ebook ISBN 978-0-593-59946-4

Library of Congress Cataloging-in-Publication Data
is available.

Printed in China

Editors: SARAH MALARKEY AND ANNE GROELL
Editorial assistant: LYDIA ESTRADA
Production editor: MARK MCCAUSLIN
Art director and designer: IAN DINGMAN
Illustrator: BRIAN REEDY
Photographer: LAUREN VOLO
Photo production coordinator and translator: MATO HERCEG
Photo location hosts: DANKA AND IVICA GIRČIĆ
Photo production assistant on location: DIEGO SENIOR
Food stylist: MARIANA VELÁSQUEZ
Food stylist assistant: INES FRANKFURT
Props: MAEVE SHERIDAN
Production manager: JESSICA HEIM
Compositors: MERRI ANN MORRELL AND NICK PATTON
Copyeditor: CLARE LING
Proofreaders: ANDREA PEABBLES, JACOB SAMMON, AND HELEN MACDONALD
Indexer: ELIZABETH T. PARSON
Publicist: LAUREN EALY

10 9 8 7 6 5 4 3 2 1

First Edition